# Norway Travel

## Discover the Land of Fjords & Adventures

**J. Dierssen**

Brief history of Norway.................................................. 10

Introduction to Norwegian culture and traditions ..................... 14

Exploring the ancient Viking heritage ........................................ 19

Traditional Norwegian art and craftsmanship........................... 22

Immersion in Norwegian folklore and mythology..................... 26

Tracing the Sami culture and traditions ..................................... 30

Northern Lights Travel Guide Norway........................................ 33

  Understanding the science behind the Northern Lights........ 33

  Best locations in Norway for Northern Lights viewing .......... 37

  Tips for capturing the perfect Northern Lights photographs. 41

  Chasing the Northern Lights on snowmobiles and dog sledding ................................................................................. 46

City Travel Guide Norway ........................................................ 50

  Vibrant city life in Oslo........................................................ 50

  Must-visit attractions in Oslo .............................................. 56

  Exploring the local food and drink scene in Oslo.................. 59

Oslo's cultural and artistic hotspots ...................................... 62

The charm of Bergen ............................................. 66

Exploring Bryggen - Bergen's historic waterfront .................. 72

Bergen's scenic fjord tours and outdoor activities ................ 76

Bergen's music and festival scene ............................................ 79

Visiting Nidaros Cathedral - Norway's national shrine .......... 87

Exploring Trondheim's historical landmarks ......................... 93

Trondheim's vibrant student life and modern attractions ..... 95

Zoos and Amusement Parks ..................................................... 144

Sørlandets Kunstmuseum (Southern Norway Art Museum),

Kristiansand ...................................................................... 144

Østfoldbadet, Askim ............................................................ 148

Ålesund Akvarium, Ålesund ................................................. 152

Norsk Bergverksmuseum (Norwegian Mining Museum),

Kongsberg ......................................................................... 156

Anno Norsk Skogmuseum (Norwegian Forest Museum),

Elverum .............................................................. 160

Norsk Romfartssenter (Norwegian Space Center), Andøya . 163

Kjuttaviga Fuglereservat, Skudeneshavn ........................... 166

Norsk Teknisk Museum (Norwegian Museum of Science and

Technology), Oslo ................................................. 168

Akvariet i Bergen (The Aquarium in Bergen), Bergen .......... 171

Vitensenteret Innlandet (Science Center Innlandet), Gjøvik 174

VilVite Senteret, Bergen .......................................... 176

Hadeland Glassverk og Krystall, Jevnaker ......................... 179

Bjørneparken (Bear Park), Flå ..................................... 181

Norsk Vilt- og Fiskeopdrettsmuseum (Norwegian Wildlife and

Fisheries Museum), Høylandet ...................................... 184

Langedrag Naturpark, Nesbyen ...................................... 187

Polar Zoo, Bardu .................................................. 189

Kristiansand Dyrepark (Kristiansand Zoo), Kristiansand ...... 192

4

Nature Reserves ................................................. 194

    Forollhogna National Park ................................ 194

    Blåfjella-Skjækerfjella National Park ................... 198

    Jotunheimen National Park .............................. 202

    Jostedalsbreen National Park............................ 208

    Øvre Dividal National Park................................ 212

    Børgefjell National Park .................................. 220

    Nordre Øyeren Nature Reserve ......................... 222

    Femundsmarka National Park............................ 227

    Lierne National Park ....................................... 231

    Dovrefjell-Sunndalsfjella National Park............... 235

Sightseeing Norway............................................ 238

Norway food...................................................... 275

    Brunost - Brown Cheese .................................. 275

    Kjøttkaker - Meatballs..................................... 278

    Raspeballer - Potato Dumplings......................... 280

Fårikål - Mutton and Cabbage Stew ...................................... 283

Rak sk - Fermented Fish...................................................... 286

Gravlaks - Gravlax (Cured Salmon)...................................... 288

Pølse med Lompe - Hot Dog with Potato Pancake .............. 291

Koldtbord - Cold Buffet...................................................... 293

Lute sk - Lute sk (Stock sh soaked in lye)............................ 296

Accommodation options in Norway..................................... 310

Norwegian cuisine and dining recommendations ............... 314

Conclusion.......................................................................... 316

Re ection on the beauty and magic of Norway ................... 316

Encouragement to explore the diverse aspects of Norwegian

culture, history, and traditions............................................ 319

Final travel recommendations and closing thoughts........... 324

Norway, located in Northern Europe on the western portion of the Scandinavian Peninsula, is a country renowned for its breathtaking natural beauty. Its geography, characterized by majestic fjords, towering mountains, and pristine lakes, provides a stunning backdrop for travelers seeking an unforgettable experience.

The country's long coastline stretches over 25,000 kilometers, dotted with countless islands and fjords that have been carved out by ancient glaciers. The most famous of these fjords is the UNESCO-listed Geirangerfjord, with its cascading waterfalls and steep cli    s that plunge into the deep blue waters below. The Sognefjord, Norway's longest and deepest fjord, is another must-visit destination for its serene beauty and picturesque villages.

Norway's geography is also dominated by its mountainous terrain. The Scandinavian Mountains, which run along the western border with Sweden, are home to some of the country's highest peaks, including Galdhøpiggen, the highest mountain in Northern Europe. These mountains o er incredible opportunities for hiking, skiing, and mountaineering, attracting adventure seekers from around the world.

The climate in Norway varies considerably depending on the region. In the southern coastal areas, the climate is relatively mild with cool summers and mild winters. As you head further north, the temperatures become colder, and the winters are long and snowy. In the Arctic regions, such as Tromsø and Svalbard, the weather is characterized by extreme cold, polar nights, and the mesmerizing Northern Lights phenomenon, making it a top destination for those seeking an unforgettable winter experience.

For cultural enthusiasts, Norway's cities o    er a wealth of treasures to explore. Oslo, the capital, is a vibrant metropolis known for its world-class museums, including the Viking Ship Museum and the Munch Museum. Bergen, a UNESCO World Heritage City, is famous for its historic wharf, Bryggen, and its lively sh market. Trondheim, with its medieval cathedral and charming old town, is a perfect blend of history and modernity.

Whether you are a cultural traveler delving into Norway's rich history, art, and traditions, a northern lights enthusiast chasing the mesmerizing phenomenon, or a city explorer seeking the vibrant atmosphere of Oslo, Bergen, and Trondheim, Norway o ers a myriad of experiences that will leave you in awe. Its diverse geography and climate, from majestic fjords to snowy mountains, provide a captivating backdrop for an unforgettable journey through the magic of Norway.

## Brief history of Norway

Norway, a land of breathtaking landscapes, enchanting fjords, and vibrant cities, has a rich and fascinating history that is intertwined with its art, traditions, and cultural heritage. In this subchapter, we will take you on a journey through the brief history of Norway, o        ering insights into the country's past and providing a context for your exploration of its art, history, and traditions.

Norway's history dates back thousands of years, with evidence of human habitation in the region as early as the Stone Age. However, it was during the Viking Age, from the 8th to the 11th centuries, that Norway emerged as a powerful seafaring nation. The Vikings, known for their exploration, trade, and raids, left an indelible mark on Norway's history and culture.

In the Middle Ages, Norway experienced a period of union with Denmark and later with Sweden, as part of the Kalmar Union. This era saw the rise of the Hanseatic League, a powerful trading alliance that greatly in        uenced Norway's economy and culture. The league's legacy can still be seen in the picturesque city of Bergen, which was a key trading hub during this time.

Norway gained independence from Sweden in 1905, marking the beginning of a new era for the country. The early 20th century saw rapid industrialization and modernization, transforming Norway into a prosperous nation. However, World War II brought dark times to Norway, as it was occupied by Nazi Germany. The resistance movement played a crucial role in Norway's liberation, and today, their bravery and resilience are remembered and honored.

In recent years, Norway has emerged as a global leader in sustainability and innovation. From its commitment to renewable energy to its focus on environmental conservation, Norway continues to set an example for the world.
As you travel through Norway, you will encounter a rich tapestry of art, history, and traditions. From the iconic paintings of Edvard Munch to the ancient stave churches, each corner of Norway o ers a glimpse into its vibrant cultural heritage. Whether you are

exploring the buzzing streets of Oslo, immersing yourself in the natural wonders of the Northern Lights, or delving into the history of Bergen and Trondheim, Norway's art, history, and traditions will captivate your senses and leave you with memories to cherish.

Join us as we delve deeper into the fascinating history of Norway, uncovering the stories, art, and traditions that have shaped this remarkable country.

## Introduction to Norwegian culture and traditions

Norway, a land of awe-inspiring landscapes, rich history, and vibrant cities, is a treasure trove of cultural experiences waiting to be explored. In this subchapter, we invite you to delve into the captivating world of Norwegian culture and traditions, o ering a glimpse into the heart and soul of this enchanting country.

Norwegian culture is deeply rooted in its Viking heritage, which shaped the country's history and values. The Norse mythology, with its tales of gods and heroes, still captivates the imagination of Norwegians today. From the stunning fjords to the majestic mountains, nature plays a signi cant role in Norwegian culture. Norwegians have a strong connection with their natural surroundings, and this appreciation is re ected in their art, literature, and way of life.

One of the most cherished Norwegian traditions is the concept of "friluftsliv," which roughly translates to "open-air living." Norwegians embrace the outdoors and spend as much time as possible exploring and enjoying nature. Whether it's hiking in the mountains, skiing in the winter, or simply breathing in the fresh air, friluftsliv is a way of life that contributes to the country's overall well-being.

Norway is also renowned for its rich folk traditions and music. Traditional Norwegian music, often accompanied by the hauntingly beautiful Hardanger fiddle, has a unique sound that transports listeners to a different time and place. Folk dances, such as the lively "halling," and traditional costumes, known as "bunads," are still proudly displayed during festive celebrations and special occasions.

When it comes to food, Norway's culinary traditions are deeply rooted in its coastal heritage. Seafood, particularly salmon and cod, takes center stage in many traditional dishes. From the famous lutefisk to the mouthwatering rakfisk, Norwegian cuisine offers a unique blend of flavors that will delight your taste buds.

In this subchapter, we will also explore the vibrant cities of Oslo, Bergen, and Trondheim, each o ering its own distinct cultural experiences. From the worldclass museums and galleries of Oslo to the charming UNESCO-listed Bryggen in Bergen, these cities showcase the best of Norwegian art, history, and architecture.

Whether you are a cultural enthusiast, a nature lover, or a city explorer, Norway has something to o er for everyone. Join us on this journey through the magic of Norwegian culture and traditions, and let the beauty and charm of this remarkable country leave an indelible mark on your soul. Cultural

# Travel Guide Norway

# Exploring the ancient Viking heritage

Norway, a land of breathtaking fjords, majestic mountains, and picturesque landscapes, is also home to a rich and fascinating Viking heritage. For travelers seeking to delve into the history, art, and traditions of this captivating country, a journey through the ancient Viking heritage is an absolute must.

The Vikings, skilled seafarers and warriors, ruled the seas from the late 8th century to the early 11th century. Their in uence stretched far and wide, reaching as far as North America and the Middle East. Today, Norway proudly embraces its Viking past, o ering visitors a chance to immerse themselves in this legendary era.

One of the best places to start your Viking adventure is at the Viking Ship Museum in Oslo. Here, you can marvel at the remarkably preserved Viking ships, which were used for both warfare and burial ceremonies. These beautifully crafted vessels provide a tangible link to the Viking Age and o er a glimpse into the seafaring life of these fearless explorers.

For a more immersive experience, head to the historical city of Trondheim, once the Viking capital of Norway. Here, you can visit the Nidaros Cathedral, a stunning Gothic masterpiece that stands on the burial site of St. Olav, the patron saint of Norway. This sacred place holds great signi    cance in Viking history, as it was believed to be the  nal resting place of their revered king.

To truly understand the Viking way of life, a visit to the Lofotr Viking Museum in the Lofoten Islands is a must. This living museum transports you back in time, allowing you to witness Viking traditions, crafts, and even partake in a traditional Viking feast. Immerse yourself in the atmosphere of a Viking chieftain's longhouse and gain a deeper appreciation for their culture.

As night falls, and the sky comes alive with dancing lights, the Northern Lights travel guide Norway niche comes into play. Imagine standing beneath the vibrant hues of the aurora borealis, just as the Vikings once did. This natural phenomenon, believed by the Vikings to be the shimmering armor of the gods, adds a mystical element to any Viking-themed journey.

Whether you're a cultural enthusiast, an adventurer seeking the Northern Lights, or a city explorer, Norway's ancient Viking heritage o    ers a captivating journey through time. Immerse yourself in the tales of these legendary seafarers, explore their art and traditions, and discover the magic of a bygone era that still echoes through the landscapes of modern-day Norway.

## Traditional Norwegian art and craftsmanship

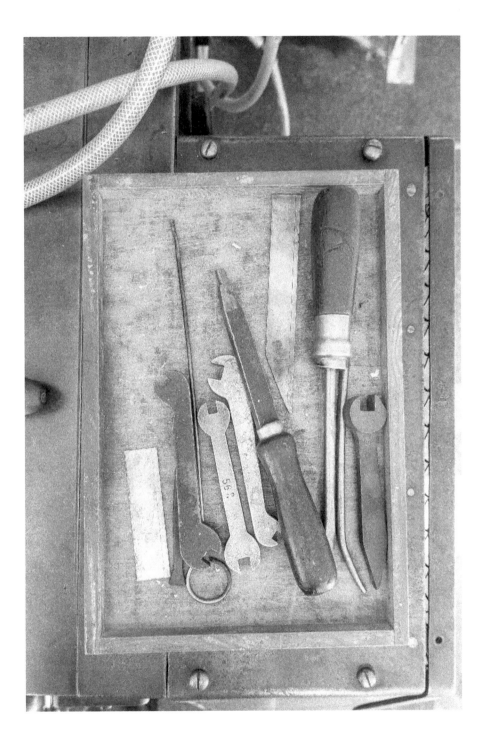

Traditional Norwegian art and craftsmanship holds a special place in the hearts of both locals and travelers alike. It is a testament to the rich history, art, and traditions of this enchanting country. In this subchapter, we will delve into the captivating world of traditional Norwegian art and craftsmanship, providing a glimpse into the cultural heritage that makes Norway such a unique destination for cultural enthusiasts, nature lovers, and city explorers.

Norwegian art is deeply rooted in the country's natural surroundings and re         ects the close relationship Norwegians have with nature. From intricate woodcarvings to vibrant tapestries, traditional Norwegian art showcases the beauty of the natural world. The craftsmanship involved in creating these pieces is truly remarkable and often passed down through generations, preserving the traditional techniques and designs.

One of the most iconic forms of Norwegian art is rosemaling, a decorative painting style characterized by intricate oral motifs. This folk art tradition dates back to the 18th century and can be seen adorning buildings, furniture, and even everyday objects. A visit to the Hardanger Folk Museum in Bergen or the Norsk Folkemuseum in Oslo is a must for art lovers seeking to explore this captivating art form.

Another notable aspect of Norwegian craftsmanship is the intricate art of woodcarving. The craftsmanship involved in creating detailed wooden sculptures, such as the famous wooden stave churches, is aweinspiring. These churches are not only architectural marvels but also bear witness to the skill and dedication of Norwegian craftsmen throughout history.

For those seeking a more contemporary experience of Norwegian art, a visit to one of the many art galleries and museums in Oslo, Bergen, or Trondheim is highly recommended. These vibrant cities boast a thriving art scene, with both traditional and modern works on display. From the iconic works of Edvard Munch at the Munch Museum in Oslo to the contemporary masterpieces at the KODE Art Museums in Bergen, travelers will nd themselves immersed in a world of artistic inspiration.

Whether you are a cultural traveler, a Northern Lights enthusiast, or a city explorer, traditional Norwegian art and craftsmanship will undoubtedly leave a lasting impression. From the intricate designs of rosemaling to the awe-inspiring wooden sculptures, Norway's rich artistic heritage is sure to captivate your imagination and enhance your journey through this magical country.

## Immersion in Norwegian folklore and mythology

Norway, with its breathtaking landscapes and vibrant culture, is a country deeply rooted in folklore and mythology. For travellers seeking a truly enchanting experience, delving into the rich tapestry of Norwegian folklore is a must. From ancient sagas to mythical creatures, this subchapter will guide you through the fascinating world of Norwegian folklore and mythology.

Norwegian folklore is a treasure trove of captivating tales passed down through generations. These stories often revolve around mythical creatures like trolls, elves, and nisse. Trolls, known for their immense strength and cunning nature, are believed to dwell in the deep forests and mountains. Elves, on the other hand, are depicted as ethereal and mysterious beings who can bring both blessings and misfortune. Nisse, mischievous house spirits, are said to protect homes and farms, but only if treated with respect.

One of the most famous mythological gures in Norwegian folklore is the legendary hero, Odin. As the chief god in Norse mythology, Odin is associated with wisdom, war, and magic. He is often depicted as a wise old man with a long white beard, wearing a wide-brimmed hat and carrying a sta    . Exploring the stories and legends surrounding Odin and other Norse gods will transport you to a world of ancient myths and legends.

To fully immerse yourself in Norwegian folklore, a visit to the countless museums and cultural centers dedicated to preserving these traditions is highly recommended. The Norwegian Museum of Cultural History in Oslo o   ers a comprehensive look into the country's folklore, showcasing traditional costumes, artifacts, and even reconstructed historical buildings. Additionally, the Stave Churches, with their intricate woodcarvings depicting scenes from Norse mythology, provide an opportunity to witness the fusion of Christianity and pagan beliefs.

If you're lucky enough to visit during midsummer, you can experience the magical celebration of Sankthansaften (Midsummer's Eve) where bon   res are lit, and traditional dances and songs are performed. This ancient pagan festival is a testament to the enduring in  uence of Norwegian folklore and mythology on the country's culture.

Whether you're a cultural enthusiast, a Northern Lights chaser, or a city explorer, immersing yourself in Norwegian folklore and mythology will add an extra layer of enchantment to your journey. From encountering mythical creatures to unraveling ancient sagas, Norway's folklore and mythology will captivate your imagination and leave you with a deeper appreciation for the rich history, art, and traditions of this extraordinary country.

## Tracing the Sami culture and traditions

Norway is a country known for its rich history, breathtaking landscapes, and vibrant culture. Among the diverse cultural groups that call Norway home, the indigenous Sami people have a unique and fascinating heritage. Tracing the Sami culture and traditions is a captivating journey that unveils the deep connection between the Sami people and the land they have inhabited for centuries.

The Sami people, also known as the Sámi or Saami, are the indigenous people of northern Scandinavia, including parts of Norway, Sweden, Finland, and Russia. They have a distinct language, customs, and way of life that have been passed down through generations. For travelers seeking an authentic cultural experience in Norway, delving into the world of the Sami people is an absolute must.

One of the most prominent aspects of the Sami culture is their reindeer herding tradition. Reindeer have been central to the Sami way of life for centuries, providing them with food, clothing, and a means of transportation. To witness this unique way of life, travelers can visit a Sami reindeer herding camp and learn about the intricate relationship between the Sami people and their beloved animals.

Another fascinating aspect of Sami culture is their traditional clothing, known as gákti. The gákti is not just a garment but also a symbol of identity and belonging. Each region and family has its own distinct style of gákti, adorned with intricate patterns and colorful embroidery. Visitors can learn about the signi       cance of the gákti and even try one on for themselves, immersing in the rich Sami cultural heritage.

Additionally, the Sami people have a deep spiritual connection with nature, which is evident in their traditional songs, joiking. Joiking is a form of chanting that expresses emotions and tells stories of the Sami people's relationship with the natural world. Travelers can attend Sami cultural events or festivals where they can witness this captivating musical tradition and understand its profound signi       cance.

Tracing the Sami culture and traditions is a rewarding journey for travelers interested in immersing themselves in the vibrant cultural tapestry of Norway. Exploring the reindeer herding camps, trying on traditional gákti, and experiencing the enchanting joiking are just a few of the highlights of this cultural adventure. By embracing the Sami way of life, travelers can gain a deeper understanding of Norway's indigenous people and their enduring connection to the land.

# Northern Lights Travel Guide Norway

## Understanding the science behind the Northern Lights

The Northern Lights, also known as the Aurora Borealis, is a mesmerizing natural phenomenon that has captured the imagination of people for centuries. These dancing lights in the sky are a result of complex scienti c processes that occur high above the Earth's surface.

To truly appreciate the beauty of the Northern Lights, it is essential to understand the science behind them. The lights are caused by collisions between charged particles from the sun's atmosphere and atoms in the Earth's atmosphere. When these charged particles, mainly electrons and protons, are accelerated by the sun's magnetic eld, they travel towards the Earth.

As the charged particles enter the Earth's atmosphere, they collide with atoms and molecules of oxygen and nitrogen. These collisions excite the atoms, causing them to emit light of various colors. Oxygen atoms emit green and red light, while nitrogen atoms emit blue and purple light. The colors and intensity of the lights depend on the type of gas particles and their altitude.

The Northern Lights are most commonly seen in the polar regions, including Norway, due to the Earth's magnetic eld. The Earth's magnetic eld directs the charged particles towards the poles, where they interact with the atmosphere to create the dazzling light show.

Travellers visiting Norway have a unique opportunity to witness the Northern Lights rsthand. The country's proximity to the Arctic Circle and its pristine natural landscapes make it an ideal destination for chasing this awe-inspiring phenomenon.

When planning a trip to see the Northern Lights in Norway, it is essential to consider factors such as the weather, moon phase, and light pollution. Clear, dark nights with minimal light pollution provide the best chances of witnessing the lights in all their glory.

In addition to the scienti c aspect, the Northern

Lights hold cultural and historical signi      cance in Norway. They have been a source of inspiration for Norwegian artists and storytellers for centuries. Many ancient myths and legends revolve around the Northern Lights, adding to the enchantment surrounding them.

As you embark on your journey to explore the rich history, art, and traditions of Norway, make sure to include a chapter on the Northern Lights. Understanding the science behind this natural wonder will deepen your appreciation for the beauty of the lights and enhance your overall travel experience.

# Best locations in Norway for Northern Lights viewing

Norway is an enchanting country that o    ers a magical experience for those seeking to witness the mesmerizing Northern Lights phenomenon. With its pristine landscapes, remote locations, and clear night skies, Norway is a haven for avid stargazers and aurora chasers. If you are a traveler with a deep appreciation for cultural exploration, history, art, and traditions, then witnessing the Northern Lights in Norway should be on your bucket list.

There are several prime locations in Norway that o  er exceptional opportunities to witness the Northern Lights in all their glory. One such place is Tromsø, often referred to as the "Gateway to the Arctic." Located in the heart of the Aurora Zone, this vibrant city o   ers a unique blend of urban life and natural beauty. Visitors can explore the city's rich cultural heritage, visit fascinating museums, and indulge in local cuisine before embarking on an unforgettable Northern Lights adventure.

Another remarkable destination for Northern Lights viewing is the Lofoten Islands. Known for their dramatic landscapes, picturesque shing villages, and majestic mountains, the Lofoten Islands provide a stunning backdrop for witnessing the Aurora Borealis. Visitors can go on guided tours, take part in photography workshops, or simply immerse themselves in the breathtaking beauty of this remote archipelago.

For those seeking a more o        -the-beaten-path experience, the island of Senja o        ers a unique opportunity to witness the Northern Lights away from the crowds. This hidden gem boasts rugged coastlines, towering mountains, and pristine wilderness. Travelers can explore the island's rich folklore, hike through scenic trails, and marvel at the dancing lights in the night sky.

In addition to these locations, Kirkenes, located in the far northeastern corner of Norway, is also renowned for its Northern Lights displays. This remote Arctic town o ers a range of activities, including dog sledding, snowmobiling, and ice shing, making it an ideal destination for adventure enthusiasts.

Whether you are a cultural explorer, a nature lover, or an adventure seeker, Norway has something to o er everyone. Witnessing the Northern Lights in this stunning country will undoubtedly be a life-changing experience. So pack your warmest clothes, grab your camera, and get ready to be awed by the aweinspiring beauty of the Northern Lights in Norway.

## Tips for capturing the perfect Northern Lights photographs

For centuries, the Northern Lights have captivated and mesmerized both locals and travelers in Norway. The ethereal dance of colors in the night sky is a sight to behold and a photographer's dream. If you're planning to visit Norway and want to capture the perfect Northern Lights photographs, here are some tips to help you make the most of this extraordinary experience.

1.      Research and plan your location: Norway o    ers several stunning spots to witness the Northern

Lights, such as Tromsø, Lofoten Islands, and the North Cape. Research these locations and choose the one that suits your preferences. Consider factors like accessibility, weather conditions, and light pollution to enhance your chances of capturing breathtaking photographs.

2.      Timing is everything: The Northern Lights are anatural phenomenon, and their appearance can be unpredictable. Check the local weather forecast and aurora forecasts to plan your visit

during nights with a higher chance of clear skies and increased solar activity. Patience is key, as you might have to wait for hours to witness this magical spectacle.

3.    Use a tripod: To capture the Northern Lights' intricate details and vibrant colors, a stable camera is essential. Invest in a sturdy tripod that can withstand the cold temperatures and strong winds. This will allow you to take longer exposure shots without any blurriness.

4.    Optimize your camera settings: Set your camera to manual mode and experiment with different settings until you achieve the desired results. Start with an ISO between 800-1600, aperture between f/2.8-f/4, and a shutter speed of 10-30 seconds. Adjust these settings based on the brightness of the aurora and the surrounding environment.

5.    Bring extra batteries and memory cards: Cold temperatures drain batteries faster than usual, so carry extra fully charged batteries to ensure you don't miss any

incredible moments. Additionally, bring multiple memory cards with ample storage capacity to capture numerous photographs without worrying about running out of space.

6.     Frame your shots creatively: While capturing theNorthern Lights, consider including interesting foreground elements like mountains, lakes, or traditional Norwegian architecture to add depth and context to your photographs. Experiment with di erent compositions and angles to create visually stunning images.

7.     Edit your photographs: Post-processing yourNorthern Lights photographs can signi cantly enhance their visual impact. Use photo editing software to adjust the exposure, contrast, and colors to bring out the true beauty of the aurora borealis.

Remember, the Northern Lights are a natural wonder that should be enjoyed with your own eyes before capturing them through the lens. Take a moment to soak in the magic, and then use these tips to create lasting memories of your incredible journey

through Norway's enchanting skies.

## Chasing the Northern Lights on snowmobiles and dog sledding

For adventurous travelers seeking a once-in-alifetime experience in Norway, there is nothing more exhilarating than chasing the Northern Lights on snowmobiles and dog sledding. This subchapter will take you on a thrilling journey through the Arctic wilderness, immersing you in the captivating beauty of the Aurora Borealis while exploring Norway's rich traditions and history.

Picture yourself gliding through the snow-covered landscapes of Norway, the crisp Arctic air lling your lungs as you zoom across frozen lakes and through dense forests on a snowmobile. The adrenaline rush of the ride is only heightened by the anticipation of witnessing the mesmerizing dance of the Northern Lights. With expert guides leading the way, you will navigate through the pristine Arctic wilderness, far away from the city lights, allowing you to fully immerse yourself in the ethereal glow of the Aurora.

If snowmobiling isn't your cup of tea, fear not! Norway o ers another magical way to experience the Northern Lights – dog sledding. Embark on an unforgettable adventure as you harness your own team of energetic huskies, who will eagerly guide you through the snowy landscapes. As you glide e ortlessly across the frozen tundra, the only sounds you'll hear are the soft padding of paws on snow and the occasional howl of the wind. The Northern Lights above will provide a breathtaking backdrop, adding an extra layer of enchantment to an already incredible experience.

But this journey is not just about the Northern Lights; it is also an opportunity to delve into Norway's rich cultural heritage. Along the way, you will learn about the Sami people, the indigenous inhabitants of the Arctic region, and their deep connection with nature. Discover their traditional way of life, experience reindeer sledding, and taste authentic Sami cuisine, all while gaining a deeper understanding of the cultural signi    cance of the Northern Lights in Sami folklore.

Whether you are a cultural enthusiast, a Northern Lights enthusiast, or simply seeking an adventure in Norway's vibrant cities, chasing the Northern Lights on snowmobiles and dog sledding is an experience that will leave you in awe. So, bundle up, prepare for an exhilarating ride, and let the magic of Norway ignite your sense of wonder as you chase the elusive beauty of the Aurora Borealis.

# City Travel Guide Norway

## Vibrant city life in Oslo

Welcome to the vibrant city of Oslo, where history, art, and traditions come to life. Nestled between the stunning fjords and lush forests, Oslo o ers a unique blend of natural beauty and urban charm. As you explore the city, you will be captivated by its rich history, awe-inspiring art scene, and fascinating traditions.

For cultural travelers, Oslo is a treasure trove of artistic wonders. The city is home to world-class museums such as the National Gallery, where you can admire masterpieces by renowned artists like Edvard Munch. Take a stroll through the Vigeland Sculpture Park, a vast outdoor gallery featuring more than 200 sculptures by Gustav Vigeland. Here, you can immerse yourself in the art and history of Norway, as each sculpture tells a di erent story.

If you are a Northern Lights enthusiast, Oslo is an excellent base for chasing this mesmerizing phenomenon. Although the city is not located within the Arctic Circle, it o     ers convenient access to the northern regions of Norway, where the Northern Lights are at their most spectacular. Join a guided tour and embark on an unforgettable journey to witness the dancing lights in the night sky, creating memories that will last a lifetime.

As a city traveler, you will be delighted by Oslo's vibrant urban scene. The city is bustling with trendy cafes, bustling markets, and vibrant street art. Explore the trendy Grünerløkka neighborhood, known for its bohemian atmosphere and eclectic mix of shops and eateries. Visit the iconic Oslo Opera House, a masterpiece of modern architecture, and enjoy a breathtaking view of the city from its rooftop.

Whether you are a cultural traveler, a Northern Lights enthusiast, or a city explorer, Oslo has something to o    er everyone. Immerse yourself in the enchanting art, history, and traditions of Norway's capital city. Discover the magic of Oslo, where the past meets the present, and where vibrant city life awaits you at every corner.

So pack your bags and embark on a journey through the captivating city of Oslo. Let the magic of Norway guide you as you explore its rich history, art, and traditions. Experience the vibrant city life and create memories that will stay with you forever. Oslo is waiting to welcome you with open arms.

## Must-visit attractions in Oslo

Oslo, the capital city of Norway, is a vibrant and culturally rich destination that o ers a plethora of must-visit attractions.

Whether you are a history buff, an art enthusiast, or simply looking to explore the city's vibrant streets, Oslo has something for everyone. In this subchapter, we will delve into the top attractions in Oslo that should not be missed during your visit.

One of the most iconic attractions in Oslo is the Vigeland Park. Spanning over 80 acres, this park is the largest sculpture park in the world created by a single artist - Gustav Vigeland. The park is home to more than 200 bronze and granite sculptures, depicting the human form in various poses and emotions. The highlight of the park is the iconic Monolith, a towering sculpture made from a single block of granite.

For those interested in history, a visit to the Viking Ship Museum is a must. This museum houses three remarkably preserved Viking ships, dating back to the 9th century. These ships, along with various artifacts, provide a fascinating glimpse into the life and culture of the Vikings.

Art lovers will not be disappointed with a visit to the National Gallery, which houses Norway's largest collection of paintings, sculptures, and drawings. Here, you can admire masterpieces by renowned artists such as Edvard Munch, including his most famous work, "The Scream."

Another must-visit attraction in Oslo is the Oslo Opera House. This architectural masterpiece is not only a venue for opera and ballet performances but also o ers stunning views of the city from its rooftop. Visitors can walk up the sloping roof and enjoy panoramic views of Oslo's waterfront and skyline.

If you are a fan of the Northern Lights phenomenon, Oslo serves as an excellent starting point for your adventure. While the city itself is not the best place to witness the lights, it provides easy access to the Arctic regions of Norway, where the Northern Lights are more frequently visible. From Oslo, you can embark on a Northern Lights tour, chasing this mesmerizing natural spectacle.

These are just a few of the must-visit attractions in Oslo. The city o    ers a rich blend of history, art, and natural beauty, making it an ideal destination for cultural travelers, Northern Lights enthusiasts, and city explorers alike. Whether you spend your days exploring museums, strolling through parks, or admiring the city's architectural wonders, Oslo is sure to captivate you with its magic.

## Exploring the local food and drink scene in Oslo

As you embark on your journey through the enchanting land of Norway, one city that cannot be missed is the vibrant and cosmopolitan capital of Oslo. Beyond its captivating art, history, and traditions, Oslo possesses a thriving food and drink scene that is sure to tantalize your taste buds and leave you craving for more.

Norwegian cuisine is a delightful blend of traditional and modern avors, with a focus on using fresh and locally sourced ingredients. In Oslo, you will nd a plethora of unique dining experiences that showcase the best of this culinary heritage. From traditional Norwegian dishes like rak    sk (fermented sh) and lute     sk (dried and rehydrated sh) to modern interpretations of Nordic cuisine, there is something to suit every palate.

One of the highlights of Oslo's food scene is its vibrant street food culture. Head to Mathallen, a bustling food hall in the heart of the city, where you can sample a variety of local delicacies. From reindeer hot dogs to freshly caught seafood, this is the perfect place to immerse yourself in the avors of Norway.

For those seeking a more re     ned dining experience, Oslo boasts a number of Michelin-starred restaurants. Maaemo, with its innovative and sustainable approach to Nordic cuisine, is a must-visit for food enthusiasts. Other notable establishments include Statholdergaarden and Kontrast, which o    er a modern twist on traditional Norwegian dishes.

No exploration of Oslo's food scene would be complete without indulging in its vibrant co ee culture. Norwegians take their co ee seriously, and Oslo is teeming with cozy cafes where you can savor a cup of expertly brewed co    ee. From traditional espresso bars to specialty co    ee shops, you are sure to nd the perfect spot to relax and enjoy a ka, the Norwegian version of a co    ee break.

To complement your gastronomic adventure, don't forget to explore Oslo's burgeoning craft beer and cocktail scene. With a growing number of microbreweries and trendy bars, you can taste your way through a wide selection of locally brewed beers and inventive cocktails.

Whether you are a cultural enthusiast, a nature lover chasing the Northern Lights, or simply a city explorer, Oslo's food and drink scene is a delightful addition to your itinerary. So, go ahead and indulge in the avors of Norway as you uncover the magic of Oslo's culinary treasures.

## Oslo's cultural and artistic hotspots

As the capital city of Norway, Oslo is a treasure trove of cultural and artistic hotspots, o	ering a vibrant and enriching experience for travelers seeking to delve into the country's rich history, art, and traditions.

From world-class museums to stunning architecture and lively cultural events, this city has something to captivate every visitor.

One of Oslo's must-visit attractions is the renowned National Gallery. Housing an extensive collection of Norwegian and international art, including famous works by Edvard Munch, this museum allows travelers to immerse themselves in the country's artistic heritage. From Munch's iconic painting "The Scream" to other masterpieces from the likes of Pablo Picasso and Vincent van Gogh, the National Gallery is a haven for art enthusiasts.

For those interested in history, the Viking Ship Museum is an absolute must-see. This museum showcases remarkably preserved Viking ships, including the Oseberg ship, as well as an array of artifacts and archaeological nds. Visitors can learn about the fascinating Viking era and gain insights into the maritime prowess and cultural signicance of these ancient seafarers.

Oslo's architectural wonders are also worth exploring. The Oslo Opera House, with its striking design reminiscent of an iceberg, is a true marvel. Not only can visitors enjoy breathtaking views from the rooftop, but they can also catch world-class performances inside. The Astrup Fearnley Museum of Modern Art, with its uniquely shaped building, is another architectural gem that houses an impressive collection of contemporary art from both Norwegian and international artists.

Throughout the year, Oslo hosts numerous cultural events and festivals that showcase the city's vibrant arts scene. The Oslo

Jazz Festival, Nobel Peace Prize Concert, and Oslo Chamber Music Festival are just a few examples of the diverse range of cultural experiences available. Travelers can also explore the city's charming neighborhoods, such as Grünerløkka, which is known for its hip art galleries, trendy boutiques, and lively nightlife.

Whether you are a cultural connoisseur, a history enthusiast, or simply a traveler seeking unique experiences, Oslo's cultural and artistic hotspots will leave you spellbound. Immerse yourself in the magic of Norway's art, history, and traditions as you explore this vibrant city and discover the hidden gems that await around every corner.

## The charm of Bergen

Nestled between seven mountains and surrounded by breathtaking fjords, Bergen is a city that oozes charm and captivates all who visit. As one of Norway's most vibrant cities, it o	ers an incredible blend of natural beauty, rich history, and unique traditions. Whether you are a cultural enthusiast, a nature lover, or a city explorer, Bergen has something for everyone.

For the cultural travel guide to Norway, Bergen is a treasure trove of artistic expression and history. The city's famous Hanseatic Wharf, a UNESCO World Heritage site, takes you back to the time when Bergen was a bustling trading hub. The colorful wooden buildings, known as Bryggen, tell the tales of centuries of trade and cultural exchange. Exploring the narrow alleyways and hidden courtyards is like stepping into a time machine.

Art lovers will be thrilled to discover the KODE Art Museums, which house an extensive collection of Norwegian and international art. From Edvard Munch to Nikolai Astrup, the museums showcase the best of Norwegian art history. The Bergen International

Festival, held annually, is a cultural extravaganza that brings together artists from all corners of the globe. It is a celebration of music, theater, dance, and literature that truly embodies the creative spirit of Bergen.

For the Northern Lights travel guide to Norway, Bergen may not be the rst choice as the city is located on the west coast, which is not the prime spot for witnessing the mesmerizing phenomenon. However, if you're lucky, you might catch a glimpse of the dancing lights on a clear winter night. For the best chances of experiencing the Northern Lights, venturing further north to places like Tromsø or Alta is recommended. Nonetheless, Bergen's cozy cafes and waterfront promenades o er a charming backdrop for those seeking a relaxing retreat after chasing the lights.

As a city travel guide to Norway, Bergen's vibrant atmosphere and diverse cityscape are sure to captivate any traveler. Strolling through the historic streets of Bryggen, exploring the sh market, and taking the funicular to the top of Mount Fløyen for panoramic views are must-do activities. The city's culinary scene is a delightful mix of traditional Norwegian avors and international in    uences, o    ering a treat for food enthusiasts. And for those seeking outdoor adventures, Bergen's surrounding mountains and fjords provide ample opportunities for hiking, kayaking, and boat trips.

In conclusion, Bergen is a city that embodies the magic of Norway. Its rich history, artistic heritage, and stunning natural surroundings make it a mustvisit destination for cultural travelers, Northern Lights enthusiasts, and city explorers alike. Whether you are wandering through the cobbled streets of Bryggen or admiring the fjords from atop Mount Fløyen, the charm of Bergen will leave an indelible mark on your heart and soul.

# Exploring Bryggen - Bergen's historic waterfront

Bryggen, located in the vibrant city of Bergen, is a historic waterfront district that has captivated visitors for centuries. This subchapter will take you on a journey through the enchanting streets of Bryggen, exploring its rich history, art, and traditions. Whether you are a cultural enthusiast, a Northern Lights chaser, or simply a city explorer, Bryggen o    ers a unique experience for every traveler.

As a cultural travel guide to Norway, it is essential to delve into the fascinating history of Bryggen. This UNESCO World Heritage site dates back to the 14th century when the Hanseatic League established a trading post here. The iconic wooden buildings that line the waterfront are a testament to the city's past as a bustling hub of commerce. Explore the narrow alleyways and charming courtyards, where you can still feel the echoes of Bergen's trading heritage.

For those seeking the Northern Lights, Bryggen serves as a gateway to the breathtaking natural phenomenon. Imagine standing on the waterfront, watching the dancing lights illuminate the night sky above the historic buildings. The combination of the aurora borealis and Bryggen's picturesque setting creates an unforgettable experience that will leave you in awe.

As a city travel guide, we cannot overlook the vibrant atmosphere of Bryggen. The district is home to a plethora of shops, galleries, and restaurants, where you can immerse yourself in the local culture. Discover traditional Norwegian crafts, admire contemporary artwork, and savor delicious Norwegian cuisine, all within the charming surroundings of Bryggen.

In addition to its historical and cultural signi   cance, Bryggen o ers a range of city-speci    c travel tips. Stroll along the waterfront promenade, take a boat tour to explore the nearby fjords, or visit the
Hanseatic Museum to gain a deeper understanding of

Bergen's maritime heritage. With its central location, Bryggen is the perfect base for exploring other attractions in Bergen, such as the famous Fish Market and Mount Fløyen.

In conclusion, Bryggen is a must-visit destination for travelers seeking to immerse themselves in the art, history, and traditions of Norway. Whether you are a cultural enthusiast, a Northern Lights chaser, or a city explorer, this historic waterfront district has something for everyone. Discover the magic of Bryggen, and let its captivating charm leave an indelible mark on your journey through Norway.

## Bergen's scenic fjord tours and outdoor activities

For travellers seeking an unforgettable adventure in Norway, Bergen's scenic fjord tours and outdoor activities are an absolute must. Known as the gateway to the fjords, Bergen o ers a plethora of opportunities to immerse oneself in the mesmerizing beauty of Norway's natural landscape.

Embark on a fjord tour and prepare to be awe-struck by the majestic fjords that surround Bergen. The most famous of them all is the UNESCO-listed Nærøyfjord. This narrow fjord boasts steep mountainsides and cascading waterfalls, creating a truly dramatic and breathtaking scenery. Hop on a boat and cruise through its crystal-clear waters, taking in the grandeur of the fjord and its surrounding mountains.
It's an experience that will leave you speechless.

In addition to fjord tours, Bergen o    ers a wide range of outdoor activities for adventure enthusiasts. Hiking in the nearby mountains is a popular choice, with trails suitable for all levels of tness. Mount Fløyen, accessible by a funicular, o    ers panoramic views of the city and is a great starting point for hikes. The stunning Vidden trail, connecting Mount Ulriken and Mount Fløyen, is a must-do for avid hikers.

For those seeking a more adrenaline- lled experience, kayaking through the fjords is an excellent option. Paddle your way through crystalclear waters, surrounded by towering mountains and picturesque villages. It's an opportunity to get up close and personal with the fjords, soaking in the tranquility and beauty of the surroundings.

Beyond the fjords, Bergen is also a cultural hotspot, with a rich history, art, and traditions to explore. Visit the UNESCO-listed Bryggen Wharf, a Hanseatic commercial district from the 14th century, and wander through its narrow alleyways lined with colorful wooden buildings. The wharf is a testament to Bergen's signi cance as a trading hub in the past.

Art enthusiasts will be delighted to visit the KODE Art Museums, which house an extensive collection of Norwegian art, including works by renowned painters such as Edvard Munch and Nikolai Astrup. Immerse yourself in the country's artistic heritage and gain a deeper understanding of its cultural identity.

Whether you're a cultural enthusiast, a nature lover, or a seeker of the Northern Lights, Bergen's scenic fjord tours and outdoor activities o er an unforgettable experience. Explore the vibrant cities of Oslo, Bergen, and Trondheim, and discover the magic of Norway through its art, history, and traditions. Plan your trip and get ready for an adventure of a lifetime.

## Bergen's music and festival scene

Bergen, known as the cultural capital of Norway, boasts a vibrant and thriving music and festival scene that is sure to captivate any traveler seeking an immersive cultural experience. From traditional folk music to contemporary jazz and everything in between, Bergen o ers a diverse range of musical genres that will leave you enchanted.

One of the highlights of Bergen's music scene is the Bergen International Festival, which takes place every year in May and June. This renowned festival attracts artists and performers from all over the world, showcasing a variety of music genres, including classical, opera, jazz, and world music. With over 200 events spread across various venues in the city, the Bergen International Festival is a must-visit for any cultural enthusiast.

If you are a fan of traditional Norwegian music, you cannot miss the opportunity to visit the Ole Bull Academy. Named after the legendary Norwegian violinist, Ole Bull, this academy is dedicated to preserving and promoting Norwegian folk music. Here, you can attend concerts, workshops, and even learn to play traditional instruments like the Hardanger ddle.

For those who prefer a more contemporary music scene, Bergen has a thriving indie and alternative music scene. The city is home to several music venues, such as Hulen and Garage, where you can catch local bands and emerging artists. These venues also host regular club nights, showcasing a mix of electronic, rock, and pop music.

In addition to its year-round music scene, Bergen is also famous for its numerous festivals. One of the most popular is the Bergenfest, a multi-genre music festival that takes place in the picturesque Bergenhus Fortress. With a lineup that includes both international and Norwegian artists, Bergenfest o    ers a unique and memorable festival experience.

For travelers interested in combining their love for music with the mesmerizing Northern Lights phenomenon, Bergen o ers a special treat. The Northern Lights Festival in Tromsø, just a short ight away from Bergen, brings together classical music and the enchanting Aurora Borealis. Experience the breathtaking beauty of the Northern Lights while being serenaded by world-class musicians.

Whether you are a cultural explorer, a Northern Lights enthusiast, or a city lover, Bergen's music and festival scene will surely leave you spellbound. Immerse yourself in the rich musical traditions of Norway, witness awe-inspiring performances, and create memories that will last a lifetime. Trondheim - A city of history and innovation

Trondheim, the third-largest city in Norway, is a captivating destination that seamlessly blends its rich history with a vibrant atmosphere of innovation. Nestled on the banks of the Trondheimsfjord, this city is a treasure trove of cultural heritage, making it a must-visit for any traveler seeking to immerse themselves in the fascinating world of Norway's past.

As you wander through the cobbled streets of Trondheim, you'll be transported back in time to the Viking era. This city was once the capital of Norway, and remnants of its illustrious past can still be seen today. One of the most iconic landmarks is the Nidaros Cathedral, a stunning Gothic masterpiece and the national sanctuary of Norway. Its towering spires and intricate details are a testament to the city's medieval glory.

Trondheim is not just a city of preserved history, but also a hub of cutting-edge innovation. It is home to a world-renowned university and a thriving tech industry, earning it the title of Norway's technological capital. As you explore the city, you'll notice a seamless blend of ancient architecture and modern design, creating a unique and captivating atmosphere.

For travelers seeking the mesmerizing phenomenon of the Northern Lights, Trondheim is an ideal base. Located in the heart of the aurora borealis belt, this city o ers easy access to some of the best spots for witnessing this magical spectacle. Imagine standing on the shores of the fjord, gazing up at the dancing lights as they paint the night sky with vibrant hues of green and purple.

Trondheim is also a vibrant cultural center, boasting a thriving arts scene and a rich tradition of music and theater. The city hosts numerous festivals and events throughout the year, showcasing both local and international talents. Whether it's a classical concert at the prestigious Trondheim Symphony Orchestra or an avant-garde exhibition at one of the city's contemporary art galleries, there is always something to captivate the artistic soul.

In this subchapter, we will delve deeper into the captivating history of Trondheim, exploring its Viking roots, medieval heritage, and the role it played in shaping Norway's destiny. We will also uncover the city's innovative spirit, delving into its technological advancements and the impact it has on modern Norway. Furthermore, we will provide practical travel tips and recommendations for exploring Trondheim, from the best places to stay to the hidden gems that only locals know about.

Whether you're a cultural enthusiast, a nature lover chasing the Northern Lights, or simply seeking to discover the vibrant cities of Norway, Trondheim is a destination that is sure to leave a lasting impression. Join us on this journey through the magic of Trondheim, where history and innovation converge to create an unforgettable experience.

## Visiting Nidaros Cathedral - Norway's national shrine

Nidaros Cathedral, located in the historic city of Trondheim, stands as a majestic symbol of Norway's rich history, art, and traditions. As the country's national shrine, it holds great cultural and spiritual signi cance, attracting travelers from all corners of the globe. Whether you are a cultural enthusiast, an avid Northern Lights chaser, or simply a curious traveler exploring Norwegian cities, a visit to Nidaros Cathedral is an absolute must.

Stepping into Nidaros Cathedral is like stepping back in time. Its origins can be traced back to the 11th century when it was built over the burial site of Saint Olav, the patron saint of Norway. The grandeur and architectural beauty of the cathedral are aweinspiring, with intricate details adorning every corner. Marvel at the towering spires, the magni cent stained glass windows, and the ornate sculptures that tell stories of Norway's past.

For cultural travelers, Nidaros Cathedral offers a glimpse into Norway's medieval history. Take a guided tour and immerse yourself in the stories and legends that surround this sacred place. Learn about the coronation ceremonies of Norwegian kings and the significance of Saint Olav in the country's religious traditions. Admire the stunning medieval artwork, including the famous Nidaros Rose, a decorative motif found throughout the cathedral.

For those chasing the Northern Lights, a visit to Nidaros Cathedral adds a touch of mystique to your journey. Trondheim's location in the Arctic Circle makes it an ideal base for Northern Lights enthusiasts. Imagine witnessing the ethereal dance of the Aurora Borealis against the backdrop of this magnificent cathedral. It is an experience that will leave you in awe of nature's beauty and the magic of Norway.

As a city traveler exploring the vibrant cities of Oslo, Bergen, and Trondheim, Nidaros Cathedral o ers a unique insight into the architectural and cultural heritage of Trondheim. Wander through the surrounding grounds and soak in the serene atmosphere. Don't forget to visit the adjacent Archbishop's Palace, which houses a museum showcasing religious artifacts and medieval treasures.

In conclusion, a visit to Nidaros Cathedral is a captivating journey through the art, history, and traditions of Norway. For cultural travelers, it is an opportunity to delve into Norway's rich medieval heritage. For Northern Lights enthusiasts, it adds an enchanting element to their quest. And for city travelers, it o ers a unique glimpse into Trondheim's vibrant past. No matter your niche, Nidaros Cathedral will leave an indelible mark on your Norwegian adventure.

# Exploring Trondheim's historical landmarks

Trondheim, the third-largest city in Norway, is a treasure trove of historical landmarks that o	er a glimpse into the rich history, art, and traditions of the country. From medieval cathedrals to ancient fortresses, this vibrant city is a must-visit for cultural enthusiasts and history bu	s alike.

One of the highlights of Trondheim is Nidaros Cathedral, a magni	cent Gothic-style church that dates back to the 11th century. This grand structure, adorned with intricate sculptures and stained glass windows, is the 	nal resting place of Saint Olav, the patron saint of Norway. A visit to the cathedral is a truly awe-inspiring experience, allowing you to marvel at its architectural beauty and delve into the city's Christian heritage.

Another prominent landmark in Trondheim is the Archbishop's Palace, which stands adjacent to Nidaros Cathedral. Built in the 12th century, this medieval palace served as the residence for the archbishop of Nidaros. Today, it houses the Norwegian Crown Regalia and serves as a museum, o        ering visitors a chance to explore its fascinating history and art collections.

For those interested in military history, a visit to the Kristiansten Fortress is a must. Built in the 17th century, this fortress played a crucial role in the defense of Trondheim during numerous con icts. Take a stroll along its ramparts and enjoy panoramic views of the city, while learning about its strategic importance in Norwegian history.

Trondheim's historical landmarks are not limited to grand structures alone. The city is also home to a number of charming wooden houses dating back several centuries. Bakklandet, the old town area of Trondheim, boasts narrow cobblestone streets lined with colorful wooden houses, giving you a taste of the city's past. Explore the area on foot or rent a bicycle, and soak in the atmosphere of this picturesque neighborhood.

Whether you are a cultural traveler, a Northern Lights enthusiast, or simply exploring the vibrant cities of Norway, Trondheim's historical landmarks o er a unique and captivating experience. Immerse yourself in the art, history, and traditions of Norway as you uncover the hidden gems of this enchanting city.

## Trondheim's vibrant student life and modern attractions

Trondheim, the third-largest city in Norway, is not only known for its rich history and cultural heritage but also for its vibrant student life and modern attractions. This subchapter will guide you through the exciting experiences that await you in this bustling city, making it a must-visit destination for any traveler seeking a combination of tradition and contemporary charm.

Trondheim is home to one of the country's most prestigious universities, the Norwegian University of Science and Technology (NTNU). With over 40,000 students from around the world, the city has a youthful energy that permeates its streets, cafes, and cultural scene. As you wander through the city center, you will encounter a multitude of trendy co ee shops, quirky boutiques, and innovative art galleries, all frequented by the city's student population.

For those interested in exploring the local art scene, a visit to the Trondheim Kunstmuseum is a must. This modern art museum showcases both contemporary Norwegian and international artworks, providing a platform for emerging artists to showcase their talent. The museum's exhibitions are constantly changing, o ering a fresh and exciting experience for art enthusiasts.

Trondheim is also a city that embraces its architectural heritage while embracing modern design. The Nidaros Cathedral, a UNESCO World Heritage site, is a prime example of the city's historical signi      cance. Dating back to the 11th century, this magni cent Gothic cathedral is a testament to Trondheim's medieval past. However, the city is not stuck in the past. The Solsiden district, with its sleek waterfront buildings and trendy restaurants, exempli      es Trondheim's modern aesthetic.

In addition to its vibrant student life and contemporary attractions, Trondheim is also a gateway to the mesmerizing Northern Lights phenomenon. As part of your Northern Lights adventure, you can embark on a thrilling chase to witness the magical dance of colors in the Arctic sky. Trondheim's strategic location, with easy access to the surrounding fjords and mountains, makes it an ideal starting point for your quest to witness this natural wonder.

Whether you are a cultural enthusiast, a Northern Lights seeker, or a city explorer, Trondheim has something unique to o    er. Immerse yourself in the city's vibrant student life, explore its modern attractions, and embark on unforgettable adventures in the surrounding natural wonders. Trondheim truly is a destination that seamlessly blends tradition and contemporary allure, leaving a lasting impression on every traveler fortunate enough to experience its magic.

# Arendal: A coastal town with a charming old town district and maritime heritage.

Nestled on the southern coast of Norway, the picturesque town of Arendal is a hidden gem that captures the essence of Norwegian coastal beauty. With its charming old town district and rich maritime heritage, Arendal o ers a unique experience for travelers seeking to explore the rich history, art, and traditions of Norway.

The heart of Arendal lies in its old town district, known as Tyholmen. Stepping into this enchanting area feels like stepping back in time, as narrow cobblestone streets wind their way through a collection of charming wooden houses dating back to the 17th and 18th centuries. Strolling through this historic area, visitors can admire the intricate details of the well-preserved homes, each with its own story to tell. Tyholmen also boasts a vibrant cultural scene, with art galleries, museums, and quaint cafes lining its streets.

For those with a passion for maritime history, Arendal o ers a fascinating journey into the past. The town was once a thriving hub of maritime trade and shipbuilding, and remnants of this maritime heritage can still be seen today. The Maritime Museum, located in a restored shipyard building, provides a captivating glimpse into Arendal's seafaring history. Visitors can explore exhibits showcasing the town's shipbuilding traditions, as well as artifacts from the days of sail. A visit to the museum is a must for any history enthusiast or maritime lover.

Beyond its historical charm, Arendal is also a gateway to some of Norway's most breathtaking natural wonders. The surrounding coastline is dotted with idyllic islands and picturesque beaches, o ering opportunities for scenic walks, boat trips, and even shing excursions. And for those seeking the mesmerizing spectacle of the Northern Lights, Arendal's coastal location makes it an ideal base for chasing this natural phenomenon.

In conclusion, Arendal is a coastal town that e        ortlessly combines history, art, and natural beauty. Whether you are a cultural traveler, a Northern Lights enthusiast, or simply someone looking to explore the vibrant cities of Norway, a visit to Arendal is sure to be a memorable experience. From its charming old town district to its maritime heritage and stunning coastal surroundings, Arendal o ers a unique glimpse into the magic of Norway.

## Arendal: A coastal town with a charming old town district and maritime heritage.

Arendal: A Coastal Town with a Charming Old Town District and Maritime Heritage

Nestled along the picturesque southern coast of Norway, Arendal is a hidden gem that boasts a rich history, a vibrant art scene, and a unique maritime heritage. This coastal town is a must-visit destination for travellers seeking to immerse themselves in the cultural tapestry of Norway.

At the heart of Arendal lies its charming old town district, a labyrinth of narrow cobblestone streets lined with beautifully preserved wooden houses. Strolling through these streets feels like stepping back in time, as the architecture re ects the town's prosperous past as a major trading port during the 17th and 18th centuries. The old town district is home to a variety of quaint shops, art galleries, and cozy cafes, making it the perfect place to immerse yourself in the local culture and indulge in some retail therapy.

Arendal's maritime heritage is deeply ingrained in its identity. The town's picturesque harbor, known as Pollen, is dotted with historic sailing ships and traditional wooden boats. Visitors can explore the Maritime Museum, which showcases the town's seafaring history through interactive exhibits and captivating artifacts. For those seeking a hands-on experience, sailing trips and boat tours are available to explore the stunning archipelago surrounding Arendal.

Art enthusiasts will nd solace in Arendal's thriving art scene. The town is home to several galleries and studios, showcasing the works of local and international artists. One of the highlights is the annual Arendal International Festival of Arts, where the town comes alive with exhibitions, performances, and workshops. This festival celebrates various forms of art, from painting and sculpture to music and theater, providing travellers with a unique opportunity to engage with Norway's artistic heritage.

Nature lovers and adventurers will also nd plenty to do in Arendal. The surrounding area oers breathtaking landscapes, with idyllic beaches, rugged cli  s, and lush forests waiting to be explored. Outdoor activities such as hiking, kayaking, and shing are popular choices for travellers seeking to connect with nature.

Whether you are a cultural enthusiast, a nature lover, or an adventurer, Arendal is a coastal town that will captivate your senses and leave you with lasting memories. Its charming old town district, maritime heritage, and vibrant art scene make it a destination that truly embodies the magic of Norway.

# Røros: A UNESCO World Heritage town known for its well-preserved 17th-century architecture.

Nestled in the heart of Norway, the enchanting town of Røros stands as a testament to the country's rich cultural heritage. Designated as a UNESCO World Heritage site, Røros is renowned for its remarkably preserved 17th-century architecture, which transports visitors back in time to a bygone era.

The town's history dates back to the 1640s when copper mining activities began in the region. As the mining industry ourished, Røros quickly became a bustling hub of trade and commerce. The wealth generated from copper mining allowed the townspeople to construct grand and stately wooden houses, which still line the streets today.

Walking through the narrow cobblestone streets of Røros feels like stepping into a living museum. The buildings, painted in vibrant hues of red, yellow, and white, showcase the traditional Norwegian architectural style that has been meticulously preserved over the centuries. The iconic Røros Church, with its distinctive twin towers, is a true masterpiece of wooden craftsmanship.

One of the town's most signi    cant landmarks is the Røros Museum, located in the former town hall. Here, visitors can delve deeper into Røros' captivating history and gain insight into the lives of the miners who once toiled in the nearby copper mines. The museum also hosts a variety of art exhibitions, showcasing the work of local artists and artisans.

For those seeking an immersive cultural experience, Røros o    ers a plethora of unique activities and events. The annual Rørosmartnan, a traditional winter market held in February, attracts thousands of visitors from near and far. This vibrant festival showcases traditional crafts, music, and culinary delights, providing a fascinating glimpse into the region's cultural heritage.

Another highlight of Røros is the opportunity to explore the surrounding natural beauty. The town is surrounded by breathtaking landscapes, o    ering numerous opportunities for outdoor activities such as hiking, skiing, and shing. In the winter months, Røros becomes a haven for Northern Lights enthusiasts, as its remote location and minimal light pollution create optimal conditions for witnessing this awe-inspiring natural phenomenon.

Whether you are a cultural enthusiast, a nature lover, or a seeker of the Northern Lights, Røros promises an unforgettable experience. Immerse yourself in the well-preserved 17th-century architecture, explore the town's fascinating history, and bask in the beauty of the Norwegian wilderness. Røros truly embodies the magic of Norway and is a must-visit destination for any traveler seeking to uncover the country's hidden gems.

# Lillehammer: Famous for hosting the 1994 Winter Olympics and its charming town center.

Lillehammer: Famous for hosting the 1994 Winter Olympics and its charming town center

Lillehammer, a picturesque town nestled in the heart of Norway, holds a special place in the country's history and culture. Famous for hosting the 1994 Winter Olympics, this stunning destination attracts travelers from all over the world. With its rich heritage, breathtaking landscapes, and vibrant town center, Lillehammer o ers a unique experience for cultural enthusiasts, adventure seekers, and city explorers alike.

The 1994 Winter Olympics put Lillehammer on the global map, showcasing its natural beauty and worldclass sports facilities. Visitors can still feel the excitement in the air as they explore the Olympic
Park, lled with iconic venues like the
Lysgårdsbakken ski jump and the Håkons Hall ice rink. Sports enthusiasts can even try their hand at skiing, snowboarding, or ice skating, following in the footsteps of Olympic champions.

Beyond its Olympic legacy, Lillehammer boasts a charming and well-preserved town center. Strolling through the cobblestone streets, travelers will be captivated by the colorful wooden houses that line the picturesque squares. The Maihaugen Open-Air Museum o    ers a glimpse into Norway's past, with over 200 historic buildings showcasing traditional architecture and cultural artifacts. Immerse yourself in the rich history of the region as you explore the beautifully recreated streets, farms, and workshops.

For those chasing the mesmerizing Northern Lights phenomenon, Lillehammer serves as an ideal base. With its proximity to the Arctic Circle, the town o    ers excellent opportunities to witness this awe-inspiring natural spectacle. Venture out into the surrounding wilderness, where the dark, unpolluted skies provide the perfect backdrop for the dancing lights. Experience the magic of the Northern Lights as they illuminate the night sky, creating an unforgettable memory.

Lillehammer is also a vibrant city worth exploring for urban enthusiasts. As one of Norway's cultural hubs, it o ers a range of art galleries, museums, and theaters. The Lillehammer Art Museum showcases a remarkable collection of Norwegian art, including works by renowned artists such as Edvard Munch and Nikolai Astrup. The Norwegian Olympic Museum takes visitors on a journey through the history of the Olympic Games, while the Lillehammer Theater hosts a variety of captivating performances throughout the year.

Whether you're a cultural traveler, a Northern Lights chaser, or a city explorer, Lillehammer has something to o er. Immerse yourself in the rich history, art, and traditions of Norway as you explore this enchanting destination. From the Olympic legacy to the charming town center, Lillehammer will leave you with memories that will last a lifetime.

# Molde: Known as the City of Roses, with beautiful gardens and scenic views.

Nestled on the shores of the stunning Romsdalsfjord, Molde is a charming coastal city that captivates visitors with its breathtaking gardens, picturesque landscapes, and rich cultural heritage. Known as the City of Roses, Molde boasts an abundance of stunning oral displays that add a touch of color and beauty to this already enchanting destination.

One of the must-visit attractions in Molde is the Molde Rose Garden, a botanical paradise that showcases over 200 di erent varieties of roses. Stroll through the well-manicured paths and let the sweet scent of the roses envelop you as you admire the vibrant colors and intricate patterns of these magni cent owers. The garden also o ers stunning views of the fjord, creating a perfect backdrop for a leisurely afternoon picnic.

For those seeking a deeper connection with nature, Molde o ers a wealth of outdoor activities. Lace up your hiking boots and embark on a scenic trek along the famous Molde Panorama Trail. This trail takes you to Varden, a panoramic viewpoint that o ers sweeping vistas of the city, fjord, and surrounding mountains. The sight of the snow-capped peaks juxtaposed with the deep blue waters is truly a sight to behold.

Molde is also a haven for art enthusiasts, boasting an array of galleries and museums that showcase the rich cultural heritage of Norway. Visit the Molde International Jazz Festival, one of the oldest jazz festivals in Europe, and immerse yourself in the rhythmic melodies and soulful performances of renowned jazz artists from around the world. The Romsdal Museum is another cultural gem, where you can explore traditional Norwegian buildings, learn about the region's history, and witness local craftsmen at work.

As the day draws to a close, don't miss the opportunity to witness the mystical Northern Lights that grace the skies of Norway. Molde, with its location in the Arctic Circle, o      ers a prime viewing spot for this mesmerizing natural phenomenon. Join a guided tour and chase the dancing lights across the night sky, an experience that will leave you in awe of nature's wonders.

Whether you are a cultural a    cionado, a nature lover, or a city explorer, Molde has something to o    er every traveler. Discover the magic of this captivating city, where the beauty of its gardens and scenic landscapes will leave an indelible mark on your heart and soul.

# Åndalsnes: Offers access to some of Norway's most famous hikes and fjords.

Nestled in the heart of the majestic Romsdalen Valley, Åndalsnes is a hidden gem that o ers a gateway to some of Norway's most breathtaking natural wonders. This small town, with its rich history and awe-inspiring landscapes, is a must-visit destination for travelers seeking to explore the beauty of Norway.

For the cultural travel guide Norway, Åndalsnes provides a unique opportunity to delve into the rich history and traditions of this enchanting country. The town itself is steeped in Norse mythology and folklore, with ancient tales of trolls and giants that still echo through the valleys. Explore the charming streets, visit the local museums, and discover the fascinating stories that have shaped this region for centuries.

For the Northern Lights travel guide Norway, Åndalsnes becomes a base for chasing the mesmerizing Aurora Borealis. With its location above the Arctic Circle, the town o ers optimal conditions for witnessing this celestial phenomenon. Imagine standing beneath a dancing sky, as vibrant ribbons of green and purple illuminate the night. Capture this magical moment and create memories that will last a lifetime.

For the city travel guide Norway, Åndalsnes provides an ideal starting point for exploring the vibrant cities of Oslo, Bergen, and Trondheim. Located just a few hours away from these urban hubs, the town o ers a tranquil escape after immersing oneself in the bustling city life. Rejuvenate amidst the serene fjords and towering mountains before continuing your journey through the urban wonders of Norway.

But perhaps the true allure of Åndalsnes lies in its unrivaled access to some of Norway's most famous hikes and fjords. The town is situated at the foot of the iconic Trollstigen, a winding mountain road that leads to breathtaking viewpoints and hiking trails. Embark on a trek through the lush valleys, hike to the towering peaks, and witness the cascading waterfalls that dot the landscape. Explore the famous

Romsdalseggen Ridge, known for its panoramic views of the fjords and mountains, or embark on a fjord cruise to experience the sheer beauty of

Geirangerfjord or the UNESCO-listed Nærøyfjord.

Whether you are a cultural enthusiast, a Northern Lights seeker, or a city explorer, Åndalsnes has something magical to o    er. Immerse yourself in the art, history, and traditions of Norway, chase the ethereal Northern Lights, or venture into the stunning natural landscapes. Åndalsnes is a destination that will leave you breathless and forever captivated by the magic of Norway.

## Aurland: A small village on the picturesque Aurlandsfjord, a quieter alternative to Flam.

Aurland: A small village on the picturesque

Aurlandsfjord, a quieter alternative to Flam

Nestled on the banks of the breathtaking Aurlandsfjord, the village of Aurland o ers a serene and idyllic escape from the bustling tourist crowds of Flam. This hidden gem is the perfect destination for travelers seeking tranquility, natural beauty, and a glimpse into the rich cultural heritage of Norway.

In this chapter, we invite you to explore Aurland, a lesser-known but equally charming alternative to Flam. While Flam may be famous for its tourist attractions, Aurland is a haven for those looking to immerse themselves in the authentic Norwegian way of life. As a cultural travel guide to Norway, we believe that Aurland o ers a unique opportunity to experience the rich history, art, and traditions of this beautiful country.

As you wander through the narrow streets of Aurland, you will be greeted by traditional wooden houses, adorned with colorful owers and surrounded by majestic mountains. The village exudes a sense of tranquility, inviting you to slow down and appreciate the beauty of nature. Aurlandsfjord, with its crystal clear waters and towering cli    s, is a sight to behold and a photographer's dream.

For the travelers seeking the mesmerizing Northern Lights phenomenon, Aurland is an ideal base. Away from the bright city lights, the village provides a dark and unobstructed sky, perfect for witnessing the dancing auroras. Imagine standing by the fjord, witnessing the ethereal colors illuminating the night sky – a truly magical experience.

While Aurland may not have the bustling city vibes of Oslo, Bergen, or Trondheim, it o      ers its own unique charm. The locals take pride in preserving their cultural heritage, and you can witness this through their traditional crafts, such as woodcarving and weaving. Visit the local artisans and learn about their time-honored techniques, passed down through generations.

Additionally, Aurland is a gateway to some of Norway's most spectacular hiking trails. Lace up your boots and embark on a journey through the untouched wilderness, with panoramic views of the fjords and snow-capped peaks. Whether you are an experienced hiker or a novice adventurer, Aurland has a trail for every level of expertise.

In conclusion, Aurland is a hidden gem that should not be overlooked. It o    ers a quieter alternative to Flam, allowing travelers to experience the beauty of the Aurlandsfjord in a tranquil and authentic setting.

Whether you are a cultural enthusiast, a Northern Lights chaser, or a city explorer, Aurland has something to o er every type of traveler. Embrace the magic of Norway in this charming village, and let it leave an indelible mark on your journey.

# Tromsø: A gateway to Arctic adventures and the Northern Lights.

Tromsø: A Gateway to Arctic Adventures and the

Northern Lights

Tucked away in the Arctic Circle, Tromsø is a vibrant city that serves as a gateway to some of the most breathtaking Arctic adventures and the mesmerizing Northern Lights phenomenon. In this subchapter, we will explore the wonders that await travelers in Tromsø, making it an essential stop for those seeking to delve into the rich history, art, and traditions of Norway.

For cultural enthusiasts, Tromsø o     ers a fascinating blend of Sami heritage, Norwegian traditions, and a thriving contemporary arts scene. The Sami people, the indigenous inhabitants of the region, have a strong presence in Tromsø, and visitors can learn about their nomadic lifestyle, reindeer herding, and traditional crafts at the Sami Center. Additionally, the city boasts a range of art galleries and museums, showcasing everything from local contemporary art to ancient artifacts, providing an immersive cultural experience.

But what truly sets Tromsø apart is its unrivaled access to Arctic adventures. From here, visitors can embark on thrilling activities such as dog sledding, snowmobiling, and snowshoeing. The surrounding snow-capped mountains and fjords o   er a picturesque backdrop for these exhilarating experiences. For the more adventurous, Tromsø is also a popular starting point for expeditions to the Arctic wilderness, where you can witness the stunning beauty of untouched landscapes and encounter Arctic wildlife.

Of course, no trip to Tromsø would be complete without chasing the Northern Lights, one of nature's most awe-inspiring phenomena. Known as the "Aurora Borealis," these dancing lights illuminate the night sky in an ethereal display of colors. Tromsø's location above the Arctic Circle makes it an ideal spot for viewing the Northern Lights, and numerous tour operators o   er guided expeditions to maximize your chances of witnessing this magical spectacle.

While Tromsø is often associated with wild Arctic adventures, it also boasts a vibrant city life. The city center is bustling with restaurants, cafes, and shops, where visitors can indulge in local cuisine, shop for traditional handicrafts, or simply soak in the lively atmosphere. Tromsø's vibrant nightlife is also a highlight, with a range of bars and clubs o ering live music and entertainment.

In conclusion, Tromsø is a must-visit destination for travelers seeking to explore the rich history, art, and traditions of Norway. Whether you are a cultural enthusiast, a Northern Lights enthusiast, or simply looking to experience the vibrant city life, Tromsø o ers an unforgettable journey into the heart of the Arctic. So pack your bags, and get ready to embark on an adventure like no other.

Stavanger: Home to the unique Norwegian Petroleum Museum and the nearby Lysefjord.

Stavanger: Home to the unique Norwegian Petroleum Museum and the nearby Lysefjord

Stavanger, a charming city located on the southwestern coast of Norway, is a must-visit destination for travellers seeking to explore the rich history, art, and traditions of this breathtaking country. With its unique attractions such as the Norwegian Petroleum Museum and the nearby Lysefjord, Stavanger o ers a truly unforgettable experience.

One of the highlights of Stavanger is the Norwegian Petroleum Museum, which showcases the fascinating history and signi cance of Norway's oil industry. As the birthplace of the Norwegian oshore oil industry, Stavanger has played a crucial role in the country's economic growth. The museum provides a comprehensive insight into the exploration, extraction, and production of oil, o ering visitors an interactive and educational experience. From the impressive exhibits and interactive displays to the guided tours and multimedia presentations, the Norwegian Petroleum Museum o       ers a deep understanding of the industry that has shaped modern Norway.

Just a short distance from Stavanger lies the majestic Lysefjord, a natural wonder that captivates travellers with its stunning scenery and awe-inspiring cli    s. The Lysefjord is famous for its dramatic rock formations, including the iconic Preikestolen, or Pulpit Rock. This at-topped cli  , towering over 600 meters above the fjord, o  ers a breathtaking view that is sure to leave visitors in awe. Hiking to the top of Preikestolen is a popular activity for adventure seekers, rewarding them with an unforgettable panorama of the fjord and surrounding mountains.

For cultural enthusiasts, Stavanger also boasts a vibrant arts scene. The city is home to numerous galleries, museums, and cultural institutions that showcase both traditional and contemporary Norwegian art. Stavanger is particularly renowned for its street art, with colorful murals adorning the walls of buildings throughout the city. Exploring the streets of Stavanger is like walking through an open-air art gallery, o    ering visitors a unique and visually stimulating experience.

Whether you are a cultural traveller, a Northern Lights enthusiast, or simply looking to explore the vibrant cities of Norway, Stavanger should not be missed. With its unique attractions such as the Norwegian
Petroleum Museum and the breathtaking Lysefjord, Stavanger o ers a perfect blend of history, art, and natural beauty that will leave a lasting impression on every visitor.

Ålesund: Known for its stunning Art Nouveau architecture and beautiful coastal setting.

Nestled on the western coast of Norway, Ålesund is a city that perfectly combines breathtaking natural beauty with rich cultural heritage. Renowned for its stunning Art Nouveau architecture and picturesque coastal setting, this charming city is a must-visit destination for travelers seeking a unique and enriching experience.

Ålesund's architectural marvels are a testament to the city's fascinating history. In 1904, a devastating re practically destroyed the entire town center. However, instead of rebuilding in the traditional style, the citizens embraced the emerging Art Nouveau movement, resulting in the creation of an extraordinary urban landscape. The buildings, adorned with intricate ornamentation and elegant facades, transport visitors back in time, o    ering a glimpse into the city's prosperous past. Take a stroll through the streets, marveling at the beautifully restored structures, and immerse yourself in the charm of this architectural gem.

But Ålesund isn't just about its magni cent buildings; it also boasts a spectacular coastal setting. Situated on a series of islands, the city is surrounded by the majestic Sunnmøre Alps and the serene waters of the Atlantic Ocean. From the panoramic viewpoints atop Mount Aksla, you can bask in the breathtaking vistas of the archipelago, the azure sea, and the towering peaks in the distance. The blend of mountains, fjords, and islands creates a postcard-perfect backdrop that will leave you in awe of nature's wonders.

For cultural enthusiasts, Ålesund o    ers a variety of museums and galleries that showcase the region's history and art. The Jugendstilsenteret, housed in a former pharmacy, delves into the Art Nouveau movement and its in    uence on the city. Here, you can learn about the architects, craftsmen, and artists who shaped Ålesund's unique architectural landscape. The Sunnmøre Museum, located on the island of Giske, provides a glimpse into the traditional way of life in the region, with its collection of historic buildings and artifacts.

Whether you are a cultural explorer, a nature enthusiast, or simply seeking a memorable travel experience, Ålesund has something to o    er everyone. Immerse yourself in the beauty of its Art Nouveau architecture, soak in the stunning coastal vistas, and delve into the rich history and traditions of this enchanting city. Ålesund is a destination that will captivate your senses and leave an indelible mark on your journey through Norway.

# Zoos and Amusement Parks

Sørlandets Kunstmuseum (Southern Norway Art Museum), Kristiansand

Located in the picturesque city of Kristiansand, the Sørlandets Kunstmuseum, also known as the Southern Norway Art Museum, is a true gem for art enthusiasts visiting Norway. This subchapter will take you on a journey through this magni cent museum, showcasing its unique collection and its signi cance in the art world.

The Sørlandets Kunstmuseum was established in 1995 and has since become one of the leading art museums in Norway. It is renowned for its diverse collection of Norwegian and international art, spanning various artistic movements and styles. From traditional paintings to contemporary installations, the museum o ers a comprehensive insight into the world of art.

One of the highlights of the museum is its impressive collection of Norwegian art from the 19th and 20th centuries. Visitors can admire the works of renowned Norwegian artists such as Edvard Munch, Harald Sohlberg, and Christian Krohg. The museum also holds temporary exhibitions that showcase contemporary Norwegian artists, providing visitors with a glimpse into the vibrant and ever-evolving art scene in Norway.

For those interested in international art, the Sørlandets Kunstmuseum o ers an extensive collection of works by artists from around the world. From modernist masterpieces to thought-provoking conceptual art, the museum presents a diverse range of artistic expressions. Visitors can explore the works of internationally acclaimed artists such as Pablo Picasso, Salvador Dalí, and Yoko Ono.

In addition to its impressive collection, the Sørlandets Kunstmuseum also hosts various cultural events and educational programs. Visitors can participate in guided tours, workshops, and lectures, providing a deeper understanding of the artworks on display. The museum also has a cozy café where visitors can relax and re ect on their art- lled journey.

For travelers seeking an enriching cultural experience in Norway, a visit to the Sørlandets Kunstmuseum is a must. Immerse yourself in the world of art, discover Norwegian and international masterpieces, and gain a deeper appreciation for the rich history and traditions of this beautiful country. Whether you are a cultural enthusiast, a Northern Lights chaser, or a city explorer, the Sørlandets Kunstmuseum will undoubtedly leave a lasting impression on your journey through Norway.

# Østfoldbadet, Askim

Located in the charming town of Askim, Østfoldbadet is a must-visit attraction for travellers seeking a unique cultural experience in Norway. As a part of our cultural travel guide to Norway, we invite you to explore the rich history, art, and traditions of this fascinating destination.

Østfoldbadet is not your ordinary swimming pool; it is a cultural oasis that combines art, history, and relaxation. The facility, which opened its doors in 2012, is renowned for its stunning architecture and innovative design. The building itself is an architectural masterpiece, with its sleek lines and contemporary style, re    ecting Norway's commitment to modernity.

Step inside Østfoldbadet, and you will be transported to a world of tranquillity and beauty. The interior is adorned with vibrant artwork, showcasing the talent of local artists. These carefully curated pieces not only add aesthetic appeal but also provide a glimpse into the region's artistic heritage.

But Østfoldbadet is not just about admiring art; it o ers a wide range of activities for visitors of all ages. Dive into the crystal-clear waters of the swimming pool, relax in the saunas, or enjoy a rejuvenating massage at the spa. For the more adventurous travellers, the facility also features thrilling water slides and a state-of-the-art tness center.

As a Northern Lights travel guide to Norway, we understand that experiencing the mesmerizing aurora borealis is a top priority for many travellers. Østfoldbadet is strategically located in the heart of
Askim, making it an ideal base for chasing the elusive Northern Lights. After a day of exploring the town's charming streets and immersing yourself in its rich culture, you can return to Østfoldbadet and unwind as you search the skies for the enchanting dance of the Northern Lights.

If you are a city traveller, Østfoldbadet o       ers a unique perspective on Norwegian city life. While Oslo, Bergen, and Trondheim are undoubtedly vibrant cities, Askim provides a refreshing alternative. Here, you can embrace the slower pace of life, connect with the local community, and discover the hidden gems that only a smaller town can o    er. Østfoldbadet serves as a cultural hub, bringing together locals and travellers alike, fostering a sense of community and providing a space for cultural exchange.

In conclusion, Østfoldbadet in Askim is a testament to Norway's commitment to art, history, and traditions.
Whether you are a cultural enthusiast, Northern
Lights chaser, or city explorer, this destination has something to
o      er everyone. Experience the magic of Østfoldbadet and let it leave an indelible mark on your journey through the wonders of Norway.

# Ålesund Akvarium, Ålesund

Located in the picturesque coastal town of Ålesund, the Ålesund Akvarium is a must-visit destination for travelers seeking to explore the rich marine life of Norway. Nestled amidst the breathtaking fjords and majestic mountains, this enchanting aquarium o ers a unique and immersive experience for both adults and children alike.

As a cultural travel guide, we believe that understanding the natural wonders of a country is an essential part of exploring its history and traditions. The Ålesund Akvarium perfectly encapsulates this idea by showcasing the diverse and awe-inspiring marine ecosystem of Norway. From vibrant tropical sh to mysterious deep-sea creatures, visitors will have the opportunity to witness the fascinating biodiversity that thrives in the Norwegian waters.

For those embarking on a Northern Lights adventure, the Ålesund Akvarium provides a captivating prelude to the mesmerizing displays of the aurora borealis. The aquarium's exhibits not only educate visitors about the Northern Lights phenomenon but also shed light on the scienti c explanations behind this breathtaking natural spectacle. It serves as a perfect introduction to the wonders that await travelers in the northern regions of Norway.

As a city travel guide, we understand the importance of discovering the hidden gems within vibrant cities. Ålesund, with its unique Art Nouveau architecture, is a city that perfectly balances modernity with tradition. The Ålesund Akvarium not only complements the city's architectural beauty but also o ers an opportunity to delve into its rich maritime history. Through interactive exhibits and educational displays, visitors can learn about the city's seafaring heritage and the close relationship between the people of Ålesund and the ocean.

Whether you are a cultural enthusiast, a Northern Lights chaser, or simply a traveler seeking to explore the vibrant cities of Norway, the Ålesund Akvarium is a destination that should not be missed. Immerse yourself in the captivating world of marine life, gain insights into the natural wonders of Norway, and discover the hidden treasures that lie within the enchanting town of Ålesund.

## Norsk Bergverksmuseum (Norwegian Mining Museum), Kongsberg

As you journey through the enchanting landscapes of Norway, exploring its rich history, art, and traditions, a visit to the Norsk Bergverksmuseum in Kongsberg is an absolute must. This fascinating museum o    ers a unique insight into the country's mining heritage, providing a captivating experience for cultural enthusiasts, avid Northern Lights chasers, and city explorers alike.

Located in the historic mining town of Kongsberg, just a short distance from Oslo, the Norsk
Bergverksmuseum showcases the importance of mining in Norway's past and present. This subchapter of "The Magic of Norway" is dedicated to uncovering the hidden gems of this remarkable museum, catering speci    cally to the interests of cultural travelers, Northern Lights enthusiasts, and city explorers.

For the cultural traveler, the Norsk Bergverksmuseum o    ers a glimpse into the lives of miners and their families through a plethora of exhibits and artifacts. From the underground mine tour, where you can experience the working conditions of miners rsthand, to the stunning collection of geological specimens and mining tools, this museum provides a comprehensive overview of Norway's mining history. Additionally, the museum houses a unique collection of artworks inspired by mining, showcasing the close connection between art and industry.

If you are a Northern Lights enthusiast, the Norsk Bergverksmuseum is an ideal starting point for your journey. Kongsberg's location, away from the light pollution of major cities, makes it an excellent spot for witnessing the mesmerizing Northern Lights phenomenon. The museum o      ers informative presentations on the science behind the Aurora Borealis and provides valuable tips on how to maximize your chances of catching this magical spectacle.

For those exploring the vibrant cities of Oslo, Bergen, and Trondheim, the Norsk Bergverksmuseum o    ers a convenient day trip option. Just a short train ride from Oslo, Kongsberg is easily accessible and provides a refreshing escape from the bustling city life. Immerse yourself in the history and traditions of Norway's mining industry before returning to the vibrant city atmosphere.

Whether you are a cultural traveler, Northern Lights enthusiast, or city explorer, the Norsk Bergverksmuseum in Kongsberg promises an unforgettable experience. Delve into the captivating world of Norway's mining heritage, marvel at the intricate artworks, and gain a deeper understanding of the country's history. Plan your visit to this hidden gem and let the Norsk Bergverksmuseum ignite your sense of adventure.

# Anno Norsk Skogmuseum (Norwegian Forest Museum), Elverum

Located in the charming town of Elverum, the Anno Norsk Skogmuseum, or Norwegian Forest Museum, is a must-visit destination for travellers seeking to explore the rich history, art, and traditions of Norway. As a cultural travel guide to Norway, we highly recommend a visit to this unique museum that o ers a fascinating insight into the country's deep connection with its forests and natural surroundings.

The Norwegian Forest Museum is a treasure trove of knowledge, showcasing the importance of forests in Norwegian culture, history, and economy. The museum boasts an impressive collection of artifacts, interactive exhibits, and immersive displays that take visitors on a journey through time, from ancient folklore and mythology to modern forestry practices.

For those interested in the mesmerizing Northern Lights phenomenon, the museum o ers a specialized exhibition that delves into the mystical allure of the Aurora Borealis. Learn about the scienti c explanations behind this natural wonder and discover the ancient myths and legends associated with the dancing lights in the Arctic sky. The exhibition also provides practical tips on how to best enjoy and capture the Northern Lights during your visit to Norway.

As a city travel guide to Norway, we understand the importance of exploring vibrant cities like Oslo, Bergen, and Trondheim. However, it is equally important to venture out into the countryside and immerse yourself in the natural beauty that Norway has to o   er. The Norwegian Forest Museum is the perfect place to start. Elverum, with its picturesque surroundings, provides a tranquil setting for this unique museum that celebrates the country's deeprooted connection with nature.

Whether you are a history enthusiast, an art lover, or a nature enthusiast, a visit to the Anno Norsk Skogmuseum will undoubtedly enrich your understanding of Norway's cultural heritage. Immerse yourself in the captivating exhibits, participate in interactive workshops, or simply take a leisurely stroll through the scenic outdoor museum area. The Norwegian Forest Museum is an unforgettable experience that will leave you with a newfound appreciation for the country's rich history, art, and traditions.

So pack your bags and embark on a journey through the magic of Norway. Discover the wonders of the Norwegian Forest Museum in Elverum and unlock the secrets of Norway's cultural heritage, all while immersing yourself in the breathtaking beauty of this Nordic nation.

## Norsk Romfartssenter (Norwegian Space Center), Andøya

Nestled in the picturesque island of Andøya, the Norsk Romfartssenter (Norwegian Space Center) is a hidden gem for those seeking a unique and awe-inspiring experience in Norway. This subchapter is dedicated to the curious travellers who are fascinated by the intersection of science, technology, and natural wonders. Whether you are a cultural enthusiast, a Northern Lights chaser, or a city explorer, a visit to the Norsk Romfartssenter is a must.

For the cultural travel guide Norway, the Norsk

Romfartssenter o ers a remarkable insight into Norway's modern scienti c achievements. It showcases the country's dedication to space research, exploration, and innovation. As you wander through the center, you will be captivated by the interactive exhibits, educational displays, and captivating stories of Norwegian scientists and their contributions to space exploration.

If you are a Northern Lights travel guide enthusiast, the Norsk Romfartssenter o ers a unique opportunity to understand the celestial phenomenon on a deeper level. Immerse yourself in the Northern Lights Planetarium, where you can witness breathtaking simulations of the auroras dancing across the Arctic sky. Learn about the science behind this mesmerizing natural wonder, complementing your Northern Lights chase with a deeper understanding of the phenomenon.

For the city travel guide Norway, a trip to the Norsk Romfartssenter provides a perfect day trip from the vibrant cities of Oslo, Bergen, or Trondheim. Escape the urban hustle and bustle and embrace the tranquility of Andøya Island. After exploring the space center, take a stroll along the rugged coastline, breathe in the fresh sea air, and soak in the stunning views of the Norwegian Sea. This serene escape will rejuvenate your senses and o er a unique perspective on the beauty of Norway.

In conclusion, the Norsk Romfartssenter in Andøya is a hidden gem that caters to the diverse interests of travellers. Whether you are a cultural enthusiast, a Northern Lights chaser, or a city explorer, a visit to this space center promises an unforgettable experience. Embark on a journey of discovery and marvel at the wonders of science, technology, and natural beauty that Norway has to o    er.

# Kjuttaviga Fuglereservat, Skudeneshavn

Nestled along the picturesque coastline of Skudeneshavn, a small town in Norway, lies the enchanting Kjuttaviga Fuglereservat. This hidden gem is a paradise for nature lovers and bird enthusiasts alike, o ering a unique opportunity to witness the beauty and diversity of Norway's avian species.

As you step into the Fuglereservat, you will be greeted by the melodious chirping of countless birds. This protected area is home to over 200 species of birds, making it a haven for ornithologists and birdwatchers from around the world. From majestic sea eagles soaring through the sky to adorable pu ns nesting on the cli     s, there is no shortage of awe-inspiring sights to behold.

The reserve's diverse landscape plays a crucial role in attracting such a wide range of bird species. With its rugged coastline, verdant forests, and tranquil wetlands, Kjuttaviga o  ers a variety of habitats for birds to thrive. Visitors can explore the wellmaintained trails that wind through the reserve, providing ample opportunities to observe the birds in their natural habitats.

For those seeking a truly immersive experience, guided tours are available, led by knowledgeable local experts. These guides will not only help you spot and identify various bird species but also provide valuable insights into their behaviors and ecological signi cance. Whether you are a seasoned birder or a novice enthusiast, their expertise will enrich your visit to Kjuttaviga Fuglereservat.

Beyond its natural beauty, the reserve also holds cultural and historical signi cance. The nearby town of Skudeneshavn is a charming coastal settlement with a rich seafaring heritage. Its quaint streets are lined with beautifully preserved wooden houses, o ering a glimpse into Norway's maritime past. Exploring the town's museums and art galleries will provide a deeper understanding of the region's history and traditions.

For travelers seeking a unique and enriching experience, a visit to Kjuttaviga Fuglereservat is a must. Whether you are a cultural enthusiast, a Northern Lights chaser, or a city explorer, this hidden gem o ers a remarkable opportunity to connect with nature, uncover Norway's rich history, and witness the wonders of its avian inhabitants. So, pack your binoculars, lace up your hiking boots, and embark on a journey through the magic of Kjuttaviga Fuglereservat.

## Norsk Teknisk Museum (Norwegian Museum of Science and Technology), Oslo

Located in the heart of Oslo, the Norsk Teknisk Museum (Norwegian Museum of Science and Technology) is a treasure trove for those interested in exploring the rich history, art, and traditions of Norway. This renowned museum showcases the country's impressive contributions to science, technology, and innovation, making it a must-visit destination for cultural travelers seeking to delve into Norway's fascinating past.

As you step into the museum, you will be transported back in time to witness the incredible advancements made by Norwegian scientists and inventors. The museum boasts an extensive collection of artifacts, interactive exhibits, and informative displays that highlight the various elds of science and technology that have shaped Norway's development.

One of the highlights of the museum is its exhibition on maritime history. Norway's strong connection to the sea is evident in this section, where you can explore the evolution of shipbuilding techniques, navigational instruments, and even step aboard a full-scale replica of a Viking longship. This immersive experience o ers a glimpse into the seafaring traditions that have played a crucial role in Norway's history.

For those with a passion for engineering, the museum's section on industrialization is a must-see. Here, you can marvel at the impressive machinery and inventions that revolutionized

Norway's industries, from the textile and paper mills to the development of hydroelectric power. The interactive displays allow visitors to understand the inner workings of these inventions and appreciate the ingenuity of Norwegian engineers.

Another captivating aspect of the museum is its focus on Norway's contributions to telecommunications and space exploration. From the early telegraph systems to the modern-day satellite technology, the exhibits highlight the signi cant role Norway has played in connecting the world. You can even explore the wonders of space through interactive displays and learn about the Norwegian scientists and astronauts who have made groundbreaking discoveries.

The Norsk Teknisk Museum is not only a haven for cultural travelers but also a valuable resource for those seeking to witness the mesmerizing Northern Lights phenomenon. The museum o ers dedicated exhibits on the science behind the Northern Lights, including the atmospheric conditions that create this breathtaking natural phenomenon. For travelers interested in experiencing the Northern Lights rsthand, the museum provides valuable information and tips on the best locations and times to witness this awe-inspiring display.

Whether you are a cultural enthusiast, an avid Northern Lights chaser, or simply a curious traveler seeking to explore the vibrant cities of Oslo, Bergen, and Trondheim, the Norsk Teknisk Museum is a must-visit destination. Immerse yourself in Norway's rich history, marvel at its technological achievements, and gain a deeper understanding of the traditions that have shaped this remarkable country.

## Akvariet i Bergen (The Aquarium in Bergen), Bergen

Akvariet i Bergen, also known as The Aquarium in Bergen, is a must-visit attraction for travelers exploring the vibrant city of Bergen in Norway. This subchapter will take you on a fascinating journey through the wonders of this marine paradise, showcasing the unique marine life and providing insights into Norway's commitment to environmental conservation.

Located on the shore of Nordnes, The Aquarium in Bergen is one of the largest and most renowned aquariums in Northern Europe. It o ers an incredible opportunity to explore the diverse marine ecosystems found along the Norwegian coast. From the mesmerizing underwater tunnels to the interactive exhibits, this place is a treat for both adults and children alike.

Step inside and discover a world of aquatic wonders, where you can witness the beauty of the Nordic sea creatures up close. The aquarium houses over 60 tanks, each showcasing a di erent species and o ering valuable information about their habitats and behaviors. From colorful tropical sh to majestic sea lions, you'll nd a wide variety of marine life that will leave you in awe.

One of the highlights of The Aquarium in Bergen is the famous Penguin Park, home to a colony of adorable penguins. Watch them waddle, swim, and play in their specially designed habitat – an experience that is bound to bring a smile to your face. Additionally, the aquarium o ers daily feeding sessions and informative talks, allowing visitors to learn more about the animals and their conservation e orts.

Beyond its captivating displays, The Aquarium in Bergen also plays a crucial role in marine research and conservation. With a focus on sustainability and education, the aquarium aims to raise awareness about the importance of protecting our oceans and preserving marine biodiversity. Through their various initiatives and partnerships, they actively contribute to the preservation of Norway's rich marine heritage.

Whether you're a cultural enthusiast, a nature lover, or simply seeking an unforgettable experience, The Aquarium in Bergen should not be missed. Immerse yourself in the enchanting world of marine life, gain a deeper understanding of Norway's commitment to environmental conservation, and create lasting memories at this captivating attraction in the heart of Bergen.

# Vitensenteret Innlandet (Science Center Innlandet), Gjøvik

Vitensenteret Innlandet (Science Center Innlandet), located in Gjøvik, is a fascinating destination for travellers seeking to explore the rich history, art, and traditions of Norway. This unique attraction o ers a wide range of interactive exhibits and activities that engage visitors of all ages in the wonders of science and technology.

For those interested in the cultural heritage of Norway, Vitensenteret Innlandet provides a captivating experience that combines education and entertainment. The center showcases the contributions of Norwegian scientists and inventors throughout history, highlighting their groundbreaking discoveries and inventions. Visitors can learn about famous Norwegian scientists like Kristian Birkeland, who made signi cant contributions to the eld of space physics, or explore the work of renowned artists who were inspired by scienti c concepts.

One of the highlights of a visit to Vitensenteret Innlandet is the opportunity to witness the mesmerizing Northern Lights phenomenon. As a Northern Lights travel guide, the center o ers a unique experience where visitors can learn about the science behind this natural wonder and even simulate their own Aurora Borealis using interactive displays. The center also provides information on the best locations and times to witness the Northern Lights in Norway, ensuring that travellers have the best chance of experiencing this breathtaking spectacle.

In addition to its focus on science and nature, Vitensenteret Innlandet is also an ideal destination for those exploring the vibrant cities of Norway. As a city travel guide, the center o ers city-specic travel tips and insights into the history and culture of Gjøvik. Visitors can delve into the city's rich industrial heritage, including the iconic Gjøvik Glassworks, or explore its charming streets lined with traditional Norwegian architecture.

Whether you are a cultural traveller, a Northern Lights enthusiast, or simply eager to explore the cities of Norway, a visit to Vitensenteret Innlandet is sure to be a memorable experience. This science center not only educates and entertains but also provides a deeper understanding of Norway's rich history, art, and traditions. Embark on a journey through the wonders of science at Vitensenteret Innlandet and discover the magic of Norway like never before.

## VilVite Senteret, Bergen

VilVite Senteret, Bergen: Where Science Meets Fun Welcome to VilVite Senteret, Bergen's premier science center, where knowledge and entertainment come together to create a truly immersive experience for visitors of all ages. Situated in the heart of Norway's second-largest city, VilVite Senteret o    ers an array of interactive exhibits and hands-on activities that will captivate both children and adults alike.

For the culturally curious traveler, VilVite Senteret provides a unique opportunity to delve into the world of Norwegian innovation and scienti c discovery. From exploring the wonders of renewable energy to learning about cutting-edge technologies, this subchapter will take you on a journey through the history and achievements of Norway's scienti c community.

Step into the universe of VilVite Senteret and be amazed by the numerous exhibits that await. Discover the magic of robotics as you interact with humanoid machines and witness how they are revolutionizing industries across the globe. Unleash your inner scientist at the chemistry lab, where you can conduct experiments and learn about the elements that make up our world.

But VilVite Senteret is not only for those with a scienti c inclination. For the avid Northern Lights chaser, this subchapter also o ers valuable insights into the mesmerizing natural phenomenon that graces the Norwegian skies. Immerse yourself in the Aurora Borealis experience, where interactive displays and captivating visuals recreate the magic and beauty of the Northern Lights.

As part of our city travel guide to Norway, VilVite Senteret is a must-visit destination for those exploring Bergen. With its vibrant cityscape and rich cultural heritage, Bergen is the perfect backdrop for this unique science center. After a day of exploration, take a stroll through the picturesque streets of Bryggen, a UNESCO World Heritage Site, and indulge in traditional Norwegian cuisine at one of the city's many charming restaurants.

Whether you're a cultural enthusiast, a Northern Lights a cionado, or simply looking for a city-speci    c adventure, VilVite Senteret in Bergen is not to be missed. Prepare to be enthralled by the wonders of science and technology, and let VilVite Senteret ignite your curiosity and imagination as you embark on an unforgettable journey through the magic of Norway.

# Hadeland Glassverk og Krystall, Jevnaker

As you immerse yourself in the magic of Norway, exploring its rich history, art, and traditions, there is one place that stands out as a true gem in the country's cultural landscape - Hadeland Glassverk og Krystall in Jevnaker. This renowned glassworks facility has been a symbol of Norwegian craftsmanship and artistic excellence for over 250 years, making it a must-visit destination for cultural enthusiasts.

Located just outside Oslo, Hadeland Glassverk og Krystall o ers a fascinating journey through the world of glass-making. Step into their workshop and witness the mesmerizing process of transforming molten glass into exquisite works of art. From traditional glassblowing techniques to innovative contemporary designs, the skilled artisans at Hadeland showcase the evolution of glass-making over the centuries.

The glassworks facility also houses a museum, where you can delve into the history of Hadeland Glassverk and its impact on Norwegian culture. Discover the stories behind iconic glassware pieces that have become symbols of Norwegian heritage, and gain a deeper understanding of the traditions and techniques that have shaped this timeless craft.

For those with a passion for collecting art, Hadeland Glassverk og Krystall o    ers a wide range of stunning glassware and crystal products. From elegant vases and delicate gurines to intricately designed tableware, you will nd a treasure trove of unique pieces to add to your collection or to bring home as souvenirs.

As night falls and the sky comes alive with a celestial dance, Hadeland Glassverk og Krystall becomes even more magical. The facility is located in the heart of the Northern Lights belt, o ering visitors a chance to witness the awe-inspiring phenomenon. Imagine standing amidst the glow of the Aurora Borealis, surrounded by the beauty of Norwegian glass art, creating a truly unforgettable experience.
Whether you are a cultural traveler, an avid Northern Lights chaser, or simply exploring the vibrant cities of

Oslo, Bergen, and Trondheim, Hadeland Glassverk og Krystall in Jevnaker is a must-visit destination. Immerse yourself in the rich history, art, and traditions of Norway as you witness the mastery of glass-making and bask in the enchanting beauty of the Northern Lights. This hidden gem is sure to leave a lasting impression on your journey through Norway.

## Bjørneparken (Bear Park), Flå

In the heart of Norway's scenic countryside lies a hidden gem for nature enthusiasts and animal lovers alike – Bjørneparken, also known as Bear Park, in Flå. This unique wildlife park o   ers an unforgettable experience, combining the thrill of observing majestic bears in their natural habitat with captivating insights into Norwegian culture and history.

For those seeking a cultural adventure, Bjørneparken provides a fascinating glimpse into Norway's rich traditions and folklore. The park features traditional log cabins, reminiscent of the country's remote villages, where visitors can learn about ancient crafts and customs. Skilled artisans will showcase traditional woodcarving, weaving, and other traditional Norwegian handicrafts, immersing you in the country's vibrant cultural heritage.

But the true highlight of Bjørneparken is undoubtedly its resident bears. This sanctuary is home to several species of bears, including the iconic Scandinavian brown bear. As you wander through the park, you'll have the unique opportunity to observe these magni cent creatures up close, while also learning about their behavior, diet, and conservation e     orts to protect them. The park's knowledgeable guides will provide fascinating insights into the bears' lives, sharing stories that will leave you awe-inspired.

For travelers with a passion for the ethereal beauty of the Northern Lights, Bjørneparken is an ideal destination. Nestled amidst Norway's unspoiled wilderness, the park o   ers a prime location for witnessing this natural phenomenon. Imagine standing under the starry night sky, surrounded by the enchanting glow of the aurora borealis dancing above you. The park's remote location ensures minimal light pollution, enhancing your chances of experiencing the Northern Lights in all their breathtaking glory.

For urban explorers, Bjørneparken is conveniently situated near several vibrant cities, including Oslo, Bergen, and Trondheim. Whether you're strolling through Oslo's picturesque streets, exploring Bergen's historic waterfront, or immersing yourself in Trondheim's rich Viking heritage, Bjørneparken serves as an idyllic base for your city adventures. Its tranquil setting o ers a welcome respite from the bustling city life, while still providing easy access to all the attractions and amenities that these vibrant cities have to o er.

Whether you're a cultural enthusiast, a Northern Lights chaser, or a city explorer, Bjørneparken in Flå promises an unforgettable journey through Norway's art, history, and traditions. So pack your bags, embark on this extraordinary adventure, and let the magic of Norway enchant you.

## Norsk Vilt- og Fiskeopdrettsmuseum (Norwegian Wildlife and Fisheries Museum), Høylandet

For the curious travellers seeking to delve into Norway's rich history, art, and traditions, a visit to the Norsk Vilt- og Fiskeopdrettsmuseum in Høylandet is an absolute must. Located in the scenic region of Nord-Trøndelag, this fascinating museum o ers a comprehensive experience that explores the diverse wildlife and thriving sheries of Norway.

As you step into the museum, you will be greeted by an impressive collection of exhibits showcasing the abundant wildlife found in Norway's forests, mountains, and coastal regions. From majestic reindeer and elusive lynx to graceful eagles and playful otters, the museum provides a captivating insight into the country's unique ecosystem. Expertly crafted dioramas and lifelike taxidermy displays transport you into the heart of Norway's wilderness, allowing you to appreciate the beauty and diversity of its wildlife up close.

The Norsk Vilt- og Fiskeopdrettsmuseum also delves into the rich history and traditions of Norwegian sheries. Explore the development of shing techniques throughout the centuries, from traditional methods used by ancient coastal communities to modern-day sustainable practices. Discover the pivotal role of shing in Norway's economy and cultural heritage, and gain a deeper understanding of the deep connection Norwegians have with the sea.

For visitors interested in Northern Lights phenomena, the museum o ers a unique opportunity to learn about the relationship between wildlife and this mesmerizing natural light display. Delve into the folklore and mythology surrounding the Northern Lights and gain insight into how animals and nature have been in uenced by this mystical phenomenon.

As a city travel guide to Norway, it is important to highlight the vibrant cities of Oslo, Bergen, and Trondheim. However, venturing beyond the cities and immersing oneself in the cultural and natural wonders of Høylandet and its Norsk Vilt- og Fiskeopdrettsmuseum is an experience that should not be missed. From the captivating exhibits to the knowledgeable sta , this museum o    ers a unique opportunity to connect with Norway's natural heritage and gain a deeper appreciation for the country's wildlife and sheries.

Whether you are a cultural enthusiast, a Northern Lights chaser, or a city explorer, a visit to the Norsk Vilt- og Fiskeopdrettsmuseum in Høylandet promises to be a captivating and educational experience. Immerse yourself in the magic of Norway's wildlife and sheries and leave with a newfound appreciation for the natural wonders that de    ne this remarkable country.

# Langedrag Naturpark, Nesbyen

Langedrag Naturpark, Nesbyen: A Haven for Nature Enthusiasts

Nestled amidst the breathtaking Norwegian countryside, Langedrag Naturpark in Nesbyen is a true paradise for nature lovers. This subchapter invites you, dear Travellers, to explore the wonders of this hidden gem that combines the beauty of untouched landscapes with the rich cultural heritage of Norway. Whether you are a cultural enthusiast, a seeker of the Northern Lights, or a city explorer, Langedrag Naturpark o    ers a unique experience that caters to all.

For those following the path of cultural exploration, Langedrag Naturpark provides a gateway to Norway's fascinating history and traditions. Immerse yourself in the ancient Sami culture and witness their traditional herding practices. The park's Sami village o    ers an insight into the indigenous way of life, complete with reindeer sleigh rides and storytelling sessions. Discover the artistry of Norwegian folklore through captivating performances of traditional dance and music, showcasing the country's rich cultural tapestry.

For the seekers of the mesmerizing Northern Lights phenomenon, Langedrag Naturpark serves as an ideal base for your expedition. Away from the light pollution of the cities, the park's remote location provides an excellent opportunity to witness the aurora borealis in all its glory. Join guided tours led by experienced experts who will take you to the best vantage points, increasing your chances of witnessing this awe-inspiring natural spectacle.

Even if you are more inclined towards exploring the vibrant cities of Norway, Langedrag Naturpark is still within your reach. Situated just a few hours away from Oslo, Bergen, and Trondheim, this hidden gem serves as an ideal day trip or a peaceful retreat after the bustling city life. Take a break from the city crowds and indulge in the park's tranquil atmosphere, surrounded by stunning mountains, crystal-clear lakes, and lush green valleys.

In conclusion, Langedrag Naturpark in Nesbyen o    ers an unforgettable experience for travellers seeking a blend of natural beauty, cultural immersion, and proximity to the vibrant cities of Norway. Whether you are a cultural enthusiast, a Northern Lights chaser, or a city explorer, this hidden gem has something to o er everyone. So, pack your bags and embark on a journey to Langedrag Naturpark, where nature's charm intertwines with the rich history, art, and traditions of Norway.

## Polar Zoo, Bardu

Located in the heart of Norway's Arctic region, the Polar Zoo in Bardu is a unique and captivating destination that o ers a thrilling experience for travelers seeking a deeper understanding of Norway's wildlife and natural wonders. This subchapter will introduce the Polar Zoo, shedding light on its signi   cance as a cultural and educational attraction, as well as its relevance to the niche audiences of cultural travel, Northern Lights enthusiasts, and city explorers.

The Polar Zoo is not just your ordinary zoo; it is a sanctuary for Arctic animals and a pioneer in the eld of wildlife conservation. Home to a diverse range of species, including polar bears, wolves, lynx, reindeer, and Arctic foxes, the zoo provides a rare opportunity for visitors to observe these magni     cent creatures up close, all while respecting their natural habitats.

For cultural travel enthusiasts, the Polar Zoo o     ers an insight into the indigenous Sami culture, which has a deep connection with nature and wildlife. The zoo collaborates closely with the Sami people, who share their rich heritage and traditions through interactive exhibits, performances, and storytelling sessions. Visitors can learn about the Sami's traditional reindeer herding practices and even embark on guided tours to witness rsthand the bond between the Sami people and their animals.

Northern Lights enthusiasts will nd the Polar Zoo an ideal base for their adventures. Bardu's remote location, away from light pollution, provides excellent opportunities for viewing the mesmerizing Aurora Borealis. The zoo's knowledgeable sta can o er tips and guidance on the best times and locations for witnessing this natural phenomenon, allowing travelers to combine their wildlife encounters with awe-inspiring displays of the Northern Lights.

For city explorers, the Polar Zoo is conveniently situated within reach of several vibrant Norwegian cities. Oslo, Bergen, and Trondheim are all easily accessible from Bardu, making it an excellent starting point for a city-hopping adventure. The subchapter will provide city-speci c travel tips, including transportation options, must-see attractions, and recommendations for experiencing the local culture and cuisine.

Whether you are a lover of wildlife, a seeker of cultural immersion, a Northern Lights enthusiast, or a city explorer, the Polar Zoo in Bardu promises an unforgettable journey through the art, history, and traditions of Norway. Embark on a magical experience that will leave you with a deeper appreciation for Norway's natural wonders and its vibrant cultural tapestry.

# Kristiansand Dyrepark (Kristiansand Zoo), Kristiansand

Kristiansand Dyrepark (Kristiansand Zoo), located in the charming city of Kristiansand, is a must-visit destination for animal lovers and families alike. This subchapter will delve into the wonders of this renowned zoo, highlighting its unique features and attractions.

The Kristiansand Dyrepark is not your typical zoo; it is a combination of a traditional zoo, an amusement park, and a wildlife park. Boasting over 150 different species and more than 1,000 animals, it provides an immersive experience for visitors to learn about the diverse wildlife of Norway and beyond.

One of the main highlights of the zoo is the Nordisk Villmark (Nordic Wilderness) area, which allows visitors to explore the natural habitats of Scandinavian animals. Here, you can encounter majestic reindeer, elusive lynx, playful otters, and even mighty wolves. The park emphasizes the importance of conservation and education, providing a unique opportunity to observe these remarkable creatures up close while learning about their habitats and preservation.

For a thrilling adventure, head to the amusement park section of the zoo, known as "Dyreparken Sommerland." This area oers a wide range of rides and attractions suitable for all ages. Whether you fancy a wild roller coaster ride or a leisurely boat trip, there is something for everyone. The park also features various shows and performances, including daily sea lion and bird shows, which are sure to captivate audiences of all ages.

In addition to its animal exhibits and amusement park, Kristiansand Dyrepark o ers a range of accommodation options, including cabins and campsites, allowing visitors to spend the night and fully immerse themselves in the zoo experience. Waking up to the sounds of nature and the presence of wildlife is an experience not to be missed.

If you are a cultural traveler, the zoo provides insights into the history and traditions of Norway through its exhibitions and themed areas. From Viking displays to traditional Norwegian farmsteads, you can explore the rich cultural heritage of the country while enjoying the natural beauty of the park.

Kristiansand Dyrepark is easily accessible from major cities such as Oslo, Bergen, and Trondheim, making it an ideal destination for a day trip or a longer stay. Whether you are a wildlife enthusiast, a thrill-seeker, or a cultural explorer, this remarkable zoo o ers an unforgettable experience for all.

# Nature Reserves

## Forollhogna National Park

Forollhogna National Park is a hidden gem nestled in the heart of Norway, waiting to be explored by travelers seeking a unique and o -the-beaten-path experience. This subchapter will take you on a journey through the wonders of this national park, showcasing its natural beauty, rich history, and cultural signi cance.

As a cultural travel guide to Norway, it is essential to highlight the historical and artistic aspects of Forollhogna National Park. The park is home to ancient Sami settlements, o    ering a glimpse into the traditional way of life of the indigenous Sami people. Travelers can discover their fascinating culture, including their traditional crafts, reindeer herding, and joiking, a form of traditional Sami singing.

For nature enthusiasts, Forollhogna National Park is a paradise. The park boasts stunning landscapes, including vast plateaus, deep valleys, and towering mountains. The diverse ora and fauna make it a perfect destination for hiking, wildlife spotting, and photography. Keep an eye out for elusive species like the wolverine and golden eagle, as well as the iconic musk oxen that roam freely in the park.

If you are a Northern Lights enthusiast, Forollhogna National Park oers a unique opportunity to witness this mesmerizing phenomenon away from the city lights. The remote location and clear night skies provide optimal conditions for chasing the dancing lights. Imagine yourself standing amidst the tranquil wilderness, watching the sky come alive with vibrant colors - a truly unforgettable experience.

For city travelers, Forollhogna National Park is easily accessible from cities like Oslo, Bergen, and Trondheim. The park's proximity to these vibrant urban centers makes it a perfect day trip or weekend getaway. You can combine the bustling city life with the serene nature of the national park, creating a well-rounded travel experience.

In conclusion, Forollhogna National Park is a haven for travelers seeking cultural, natural, and adventurous experiences. Whether you are interested in exploring the rich history and traditions of Norway, witnessing the magical Northern Lights, or simply escaping the city buzz, this national park has something to o er for everyone. So pack your bags, put on your hiking boots, and get ready to embark on an unforgettable journey through the magic of Forollhogna National Park.


## Blåfjella-Skjækerfjella National Park

Blåfjella-Skjækerfjella National Park: A Wilderness
Retreat in Norway

Nestled in the heart of Norway, the BlåfjellaSkjækerfjella
National Park is a breathtaking wilderness retreat that o ers a
unique and aweinspiring experience for all travelers. This
subchapter of "The Magic of Norway: A Journey through Art,
History, and Traditions" is dedicated to uncovering the hidden
gems of this national park and its signi cance in Norwegian
culture and history.

For cultural travel enthusiasts, Blåfjella-Skjækerfjella National
Park is a haven for exploring the rich history, art, and traditions
of Norway. The park is home to ancient Sami settlements, where
you can learn about their nomadic way of life and traditional
reindeer herding. Immerse yourself in the Sami culture through
storytelling, music, and traditional handicrafts. The park also
boasts ancient rock carvings, giving visitors a glimpse into the
lives of early settlers in the region.

For those seeking the mesmerizing phenomenon of the Northern Lights, Blåfjella-Skjækerfjella National Park o ers an ideal location. Away from the city lights, the park provides the perfect backdrop for witnessing the dancing colors of the Aurora Borealis. With its vast expanse of unspoiled nature, you can chase the Northern Lights through the snowy valleys, frozen lakes, and towering mountains, creating memories that will last a lifetime.

Blåfjella-Skjækerfjella National Park is not just a haven for nature enthusiasts; it also o      ers vibrant city experiences. The park is conveniently located near the cities of Oslo, Bergen, and Trondheim, making it an excellent addition to any city travel guide. After exploring the bustling streets and cultural attractions of these vibrant cities, escape to the tranquility of the national park. Enjoy outdoor activities such as hiking, skiing, and wildlife spotting, all within a short distance from the city centers.

Whether you are a cultural traveler, a Northern Lights enthusiast, or a city explorer, Blåfjella-Skjækerfjella National Park has something for everyone. Its unique blend of natural beauty, cultural signi cance, and proximity to vibrant cities make it a must-visit destination in Norway. Immerse yourself in the magic of this wilderness retreat and discover the true essence of Norway.

## Jotunheimen National Park

Jotunheimen National Park: A Majestic Haven for
Nature and Adventure

Nestled in the heart of Norway, Jotunheimen National Park is a
natural wonderland that captivates the hearts of both nature
enthusiasts and adventure seekers. With its striking landscapes,
majestic peaks, and pristine wilderness, this park o ers a unique
and awe-inspiring experience for travelers.

For the cultural travel guide to Norway, Jotunheimen National
Park is a treasure trove of history and ancient traditions. Its
name translates to "Home of the Giants," derived from the
Norse mythology that once reigned in this region. The park is
steeped in folklore and legends, with tales of giants, trolls, and
mythical creatures that have been passed down through
generations. Exploring the park allows visitors to immerse
themselves in the rich cultural heritage of Norway and witness
its deep connection to the land.

For the Northern Lights travel guide to Norway, Jotunheimen National Park o   ers a unique opportunity to witness the mesmerizing dance of the Aurora Borealis. Away from the city lights, the park provides a perfect backdrop for experiencing this celestial phenomenon. Imagine standing beneath the starry night sky, surrounded by snow-covered peaks, as the vibrant colors of the Northern Lights illuminate the horizon. It is a truly magical and unforgettable experience.

For the city travel guide to Norway, Jotunheimen National Park

o       ers a peaceful retreat from the bustling cities of Oslo,

Bergen, and Trondheim. Located just a few hours away from

these vibrant urban centers, the park provides a perfect escape

into nature. Whether it's hiking, climbing, or skiing,

Jotunheimen o      ers a wide range of outdoor activities for

adventure enthusiasts. From the iconic Besseggen Ridge hike to

cross-country skiing in the winter, the park caters to all levels of

tness and interests.


In addition to its breathtaking landscapes,

Jotunheimen National Park is also home to a diverse range of

ora and fauna. The park boasts an abundance of wildlife,

including reindeer, arctic foxes, and golden eagles. It is also a

haven for birdwatchers, with numerous species of birds

migrating through the area.

Whether you are seeking cultural immersion, a rendezvous with the Northern Lights, or an adventurous escape into nature, Jotunheimen National Park has it all. Embrace the magic of this enchanting destination and let it leave an indelible mark on your journey through Norway.

## Jostedalsbreen National Park

Jostedalsbreen National Park: Exploring Norway's
Glacial Beauty

Nestled in the heart of Norway, Jostedalsbreen National Park is a must-visit destination for travellers seeking to immerse themselves in the cultural and natural wonders of this Scandinavian gem. As the largest glacier in mainland Europe, Jostedalsbreen o ers a breathtaking backdrop of snow-capped peaks, shimmering ice elds, and crystal-clear blue lakes. This subchapter of "The Magic of Norway: A Journey through Art, History, and Traditions" will transport you to this enchanting national park, catering to the interests of cultural explorers, Northern Lights enthusiasts, and city travellers alike.

For cultural travel enthusiasts, Jostedalsbreen National Park is a treasure trove of history and tradition. The park is home to several ancient Viking burial sites, providing a fascinating glimpse into Norway's rich Scandinavian heritage. Immerse yourself in the myths and legends surrounding these burial mounds, and discover the customs and rituals of the ancient Norse people. Moreover, explore the nearby Jostedal Open-Air Museum, where traditional Norwegian architecture and way of life are beautifully preserved. From ancient folklore to traditional craftsmanship, Jostedalsbreen National Park o ers a cultural experience like no other.

Northern Lights enthusiasts will be captivated by the mesmerizing display of nature's nest light show. Nestled under clear, dark skies, Jostedalsbreen National Park provides an ideal setting to witness the elusive Northern Lights dance across the horizon. Join a guided tour and chase the ethereal glow, as the vibrant colors of green, pink, and purple cascade overhead. Capture this magical phenomenon through the lens of your camera and create memories that will last a lifetime.

City travellers will nd Jostedalsbreen National Park a welcome respite from the bustling urban centers of Oslo, Bergen, and Trondheim. Just a short drive from these vibrant cities, the park o ers a serene and picturesque escape from the hustle and bustle. Take in the stunning views of the glacier as you hike through pristine valleys, or embark on a thrilling glacier walk led by experienced guides. For those seeking adventure, indulge in adrenaline-pumping activities such as ice climbing or kayaking in the glacier-fed rivers. Jostedalsbreen National Park truly o ers a unique blend of natural beauty and urban accessibility.

Whether you are a cultural enthusiast, Northern Lights chaser, or city traveller, Jostedalsbreen National Park is a destination that promises to captivate your senses. Immerse yourself in Norway's rich history, witness nature's most captivating light show, or simply nd solace amidst the breathtaking glacial landscapes. Jostedalsbreen National Park is the epitome of Norway's magic, waiting to be explored.

# Øvre Dividal National Park

Øvre Dividal National Park: A Wilderness Haven in Norway

Nestled in the picturesque region of Troms County, Øvre Dividal National Park is a true gem for nature enthusiasts and adventure seekers. Spanning over 750 square kilometers, this pristine wilderness is a haven for wildlife, o ering breathtaking landscapes and a glimpse into Norway's natural wonders. Whether you are a cultural traveler, a Northern Lights enthusiast, or a city explorer, a visit to Øvre Dividal National Park is an experience not to be missed.

For cultural travelers, Øvre Dividal National Park provides a unique opportunity to immerse oneself in the rich history and traditions of Norway. The park is home to the indigenous Sami people, who have inhabited these lands for centuries. Visitors can learn about their way of life, traditional reindeer herding, and even try their hand at Sami handicrafts. The park also hosts cultural events and festivals throughout the year, showcasing Sami music, dance, and cuisine, providing a truly immersive cultural experience.

Northern Lights enthusiasts will be captivated by the magic that dances across the night sky in Øvre Dividal National Park. With its remote location and low light pollution, the park o     ers optimal conditions for witnessing the mesmerizing Northern Lights phenomenon. Imagine standing under a star-studded sky, as vibrant ribbons of green, purple, and pink illuminate the darkness. Joining a guided tour or camping in the park's designated areas will increase your chances of witnessing this ethereal spectacle.

For city explorers, Øvre Dividal National Park is a perfect getaway from the vibrant cities of Oslo, Bergen, and Trondheim. Just a short drive or train ride away, the park o     ers a serene retreat into nature's embrace. Hiking trails wind through ancient forests, crystal-clear rivers, and dramatic mountain peaks, providing a thrilling adventure for outdoor enthusiasts. Camping facilities and cozy cabins are available for those wanting to spend more time in this untouched wilderness.

Whether you are seeking cultural immersion, a chance to witness the Northern Lights, or a break from city life, Øvre Dividal National Park has something to o     er every traveler. Its untouched beauty, rich history, and stunning landscapes make it a must-visit destination in Norway. So pack your bags, embrace the spirit of adventure, and embark on a journey through this magical national park.

# Børgefjell National Park

Børgefjell National Park: A Hidden Gem for Nature
Enthusiasts

Nestled in the heart of Norway, Børgefjell National Park is a
breathtaking destination that captivates the senses and o ers a
truly immersive experience for travelers seeking to connect with
nature. This subchapter will introduce you to the wonders of
Børgefjell National Park, its rich history, stunning art, and ancient
traditions that have shaped this enchanting region.

For cultural travel enthusiasts, Børgefjell National
Park presents a unique opportunity to explore Norway's ancient
history. The park is home to numerous archaeological sites,
including rock carvings and ancient settlements dating back
thousands of years. Immerse yourself in the rich cultural heritage
of the Sami people, the indigenous population of this region, as
you discover their traditional way of life, music, and handicrafts.

If you are a Northern Lights enthusiast, Børgefjell National Park is a must-visit destination. Its remote location and minimal light pollution make it an ideal spot for witnessing the mesmerizing dance of the Aurora Borealis. Imagine standing amidst the serene beauty of snow-covered landscapes, gazing up at the vibrant colors of the Northern Lights as they illuminate the night sky – an experience that will leave you in awe.

For those who prefer city exploration, Børgefjell National Park o ers a gateway to vibrant Norwegian cities. Oslo, Bergen, and Trondheim are all within close proximity, making it convenient for travelers to combine their visit to the park with a city adventure. Discover the cultural treasures of Oslo, stroll through the colorful streets of Bergen, or immerse yourself in the medieval charm of Trondheim. Our city travel guide provides you with insider tips, ensuring you make the most of your urban explorations.

In addition to its cultural and city attractions, Børgefjell National Park boasts an array of outdoor activities. Hiking enthusiasts can embark on thrilling trails, traversing valleys, and scaling breathtaking peaks. The park's diverse ora and fauna o    er a treat for nature lovers and wildlife enthusiasts. Keep an eye out for reindeer, moose, and the elusive Arctic fox as you venture through this untamed wilderness.

Whether you are a cultural traveler, a Northern Lights chaser, or a city explorer, Børgefjell National Park promises an unforgettable journey through art, history, and traditions. Uncover the magic of Norway's hidden gem as you immerse yourself in the natural wonders and rich cultural heritage that de ne this extraordinary destination.

## Nordre Øyeren Nature Reserve

Nordre Øyeren Nature Reserve: A Haven of Natural Beauty in Norway

Nestled in the heart of Norway, the Nordre Øyeren Nature Reserve is a hidden gem waiting to be discovered by avid travellers. This enchanting reserve spans over 221 square kilometers, making it the largest inland delta in Northern Europe. With its diverse ecosystems, pristine lakes, and rich biodiversity, Nordre Øyeren is a paradise for nature enthusiasts and a must-visit for anyone seeking to explore the natural wonders of Norway.

For cultural travel enthusiasts, Nordre Øyeren Nature Reserve o	ers a unique opportunity to delve into Norway's rich history. The reserve is home to several ancient burial mounds, showcasing the region's ancient past. These burial mounds, dating back to the Iron Age, provide a glimpse into the rituals and traditions of the early Norwegian settlers. Exploring these archaeological sites is like stepping back in time and immersing oneself in the country's fascinating heritage.

Northern Lights enthusiasts will be captivated by the mystical beauty that unfolds in Nordre Øyeren during the winter months. As one of the prime locations for witnessing the mesmerizing Northern Lights phenomenon, the reserve o ers an unforgettable experience. Imagine gazing up at the starry night sky as vibrant hues of green, purple, and pink dance across the horizon, creating a breathtaking spectacle. Nordre Øyeren provides the perfect backdrop for an unforgettable Northern Lights adventure.

Beyond its natural wonders, Nordre Øyeren Nature Reserve is located within close proximity to some of Norway's vibrant cities. Travellers seeking city exploration will nd themselves within reach of Oslo, Bergen, and Trondheim. These cities o er a myriad of cultural and historical attractions, from world-class museums to magni cent architectural landmarks.
Whether it's strolling through the picturesque streets of Bergen, visiting the iconic Vigeland Sculpture Park in Oslo, or exploring

the medieval Nidaros Cathedral in Trondheim, there is something for everyone.

For those looking to escape the bustling city life, Nordre Øyeren Nature Reserve provides a tranquil retreat where one can reconnect with nature and unwind in the serenity of the great outdoors. Whether it's birdwatching, hiking along scenic trails, or simply enjoying a peaceful picnic by the lakeside, this nature reserve o    ers an abundance of opportunities to recharge and rejuvenate.

As a cultural travel guide, Northern Lights travel guide, or city travel guide in Norway, exploring Nordre Øyeren Nature Reserve promises an unforgettable adventure. From its rich history and cultural signi cance to its mesmerizing Northern Lights displays and proximity to vibrant cities, this hidden gem has something to o    er every traveller seeking to immerse themselves in the magic of Norway.

# Femundsmarka National Park

# Femundsmarka National Park: A Wilderness Haven in Norway

For the intrepid traveller seeking to explore the natural wonders of Norway, Femundsmarka National Park is an absolute must-visit destination. Located in the heart of the country, this pristine wilderness o    ers a unique blend of breathtaking landscapes, rich history, and fascinating traditions that will captivate cultural enthusiasts, northern lights chasers, and city explorers alike.

Covering an expansive area of over 577 square miles, Femundsmarka National Park is a haven for nature lovers. Towering mountains, deep valleys, and crystal-clear lakes dot the park, creating a picturesque backdrop for outdoor adventures. Hiking enthusiasts can embark on thrilling trails that wind through ancient forests, across wild    ower meadows, and up to panoramic viewpoints that oer aweinspiring vistas of the surrounding wilderness.

But Femundsmarka National Park is more than just a natural paradise. It also boasts a rich history that dates back thousands of years. The park has been inhabited by the indigenous Sami people for centuries, and their traditional way of life is still evident in the region. Travellers can learn about their reindeer herding practices, intricate handicrafts, and unique cultural traditions through immersive experiences and guided tours.

For those enchanted by the mesmerizing Northern Lights phenomenon, Femundsmarka National Park is a prime location for chasing these elusive lights. With its remote location and minimal light pollution, the park o    ers the perfect conditions for witnessing nature's most dazzling light show. Visitors can join expert guides who will lead them to the best viewing spots and provide insights into the science and folklore behind the Northern Lights.

While Femundsmarka National Park is a nature lover's paradise, it is also conveniently located near some of Norway's vibrant cities. Travellers can easily combine their wilderness adventures with a visit to Oslo, Bergen, or Trondheim, each o ering its own unique cultural experiences. From world-class museums and art galleries to trendy restaurants and bustling markets, these cities are a treasure trove of Norwegian history, art, and traditions.

In conclusion, Femundsmarka National Park is a true gem in Norway's crown, o ering a diverse range of experiences for travellers. Whether you are seeking a cultural immersion, a chance to witness the Northern Lights, or an exploration of Norway's vibrant cities, this national park has it all. Discover the magic of Femundsmarka and let its wild beauty and rich heritage leave an indelible mark on your travel memories.

## Lierne National Park

Lierne National Park: Where Nature and Culture Unite

Nestled in the heart of Norway, Lierne National Park is a hidden gem that perfectly encapsulates the magic of this beautiful country. From its sprawling forests and majestic mountains to its rich cultural heritage, Lierne National Park o ers a truly unforgettable experience for travelers seeking to delve into the art, history, and traditions of Norway.

For cultural enthusiasts, Lierne National Park presents a unique opportunity to explore the rich history of the region. The park is home to ancient Sami settlements, where visitors can learn about the indigenous people of Norway and their traditional way of life. Immerse yourself in their captivating stories, folklore, and handicrafts, and gain a deep appreciation for the cultural heritage that has shaped Norway into what it is today.

For those fascinated by the mesmerizing phenomenon of the Northern Lights, Lierne National Park is a prime location for chasing these ethereal lights. Far away from the bright city lights, the park o ers an unspoiled and uninterrupted view of the night sky, where the Aurora Borealis dances in all its glory. Stand in awe as the vibrant colors paint the sky, creating a truly magical experience that will stay with you forever.

But Lierne National Park is not just for nature enthusiasts. It also caters to the urban explorer, o ering a gateway to the vibrant cities of Oslo, Bergen, and Trondheim. Whether you're strolling through the charming streets of Oslo, visiting the historic Bryggen district in Bergen, or exploring the medieval Nidaros Cathedral in Trondheim, Lierne National Park serves as a perfect starting point for your city adventures. Discover the unique blend of modernity and tradition that these cities have to o er and indulge in their vibrant cultural scenes, including world-class museums, art galleries, and music festivals.

No matter what niche of travelers you belong to, Lierne National Park has something to o er everyone. It is a place where nature and culture unite, providing an immersive and enriching experience for those seeking to uncover the magic of Norway. So pack your bags, embark on a journey of a lifetime, and let Lierne National Park be your gateway to the art, history, and traditions that make Norway truly special.

# Dovrefjell-Sunndalsfjella National Park

Dovrefjell-Sunndalsfjella National Park: A Majestic Haven for Nature Enthusiasts

Nestled in the heart of Norway, the DovrefjellSunndalsfjella National Park is an enchanting destination that perfectly embodies the country's stunning natural beauty. This subchapter will take you on a journey through this magnicent national park, catering to the interests of cultural explorers, Northern Lights enthusiasts, and city travelers alike.

For cultural travel guide enthusiasts, DovrefjellSunndalsfjella National Park o    ers a unique opportunity to delve into the rich history and traditions of Norway. The park is home to the iconic Musk Ox, a symbol of ancient Norway. These powerful creatures have roamed the area for centuries and represent a link to the country's past. Immerse yourself in the cultural signi cance of these animals by exploring the Musk Ox Center, where you can learn about their history, habitat, and conservation e orts.

Northern Lights travel guide enthusiasts will nd Dovrefjell-Sunndalsfjella National Park to be a prime location for chasing this mesmerizing phenomenon. The park's remote location and minimal light pollution provide optimal conditions for witnessing the dancing lights of the Aurora Borealis. Bundle up and embark on a nighttime adventure, guided by experts who will lead you to the best vantage points to witness this magical display.

City travel guide enthusiasts can also nd their place in Dovrefjell-Sunndalsfjella National Park. The nearby city of Trondheim, known for its vibrant cultural scene and historical landmarks, serves as an excellent basecamp for exploring the park. After a day of hiking through the park's picturesque landscapes, return to Trondheim and indulge in its bustling city life, renowned restaurants, and charming architecture.

Regardless of your niche, Dovrefjell-Sunndalsfjella National Park promises an unforgettable experience. Immerse yourself in the breathtaking scenery, from snow-capped mountains and crystal-clear rivers to sprawling valleys and lush forests. Be captivated by the untamed wilderness and the abundance of wildlife, including reindeer, eagles, and foxes.

Whether you are a cultural explorer, Northern Lights enthusiast, or city traveler, Dovrefjell-Sunndalsfjella National Park o ers a unique and diverse experience that will leave you in awe of Norway's natural wonders. So, pack your bags and embark on a journey through this magical haven where art, history, and traditions converge in the most spectacular way.

# Sightseeing Norway

Nidaros Cathedral in Trondheim, the largest medieval church in Northern Europe.

Nidaros Cathedral in Trondheim, the largest medieval church in Northern Europe

Nidaros Cathedral, located in the charming city of Trondheim, is a magni  cent architectural masterpiece that stands as a testament to Norway's rich history and religious heritage. As the largest medieval church in Northern Europe, this grand cathedral attracts visitors from all over the world, o ering a unique glimpse into Norway's cultural and artistic past.

Built over the burial site of the country's patron saint, St. Olav, Nidaros Cathedral has been a place of pilgrimage for centuries. Its construction began in the 11th century and continued for several centuries, resulting in a stunning blend of architectural styles, including Romanesque and Gothic elements.

As travelers step inside the cathedral, they are immediately captivated by its towering nave and intricate stained glass windows. The cathedral's interior is adorned with beautiful sculptures, ornate altars, and breathtaking frescoes, allowing visitors to immerse themselves in the rich artistic traditions of Norway.

One of the highlights of a visit to Nidaros Cathedral is the opportunity to witness the famous Rose Window. This magni cent stained glass masterpiece, dating back to the 13th century, depicts scenes from the Bible and Norwegian history, radiating a kaleidoscope of colors when sunlight lters through.

Beyond its architectural and artistic marvels, Nidaros Cathedral holds deep religious signi cance for Norwegians. It has been the coronation site for Norwegian kings and queens since the Middle Ages, making it a symbol of the nation's unity and identity.

For those interested in exploring the vibrant history of Trondheim and Norway, a visit to Nidaros Cathedral is a must. The cathedral o ers guided tours that provide a comprehensive insight into its history, art, and religious importance. Visitors can also attend religious services and experience the spiritual atmosphere that permeates this sacred space.

Trondheim itself is a city steeped in history and culture, with charming cobblestone streets, colorful wooden houses, and a lively waterfront area.
Travelers can combine their visit to Nidaros Cathedral with exploring the city's other attractions, such as the Archbishop's Palace, the historic Bakklandet district, and the iconic Old Town Bridge.

Whether you are a cultural enthusiast, a seeker of Northern Lights, or a city explorer, a visit to Nidaros Cathedral promises to be a captivating and enriching experience. Immerse yourself in the magic of Norway's history, art, and traditions as you stand in awe of this majestic medieval church, a true marvel of Northern Europe.

Hurtigruten, the coastal voyage route along Norway's coast.

Hurtigruten, the coastal voyage route along Norway's coast

Embark on a mesmerizing journey along the stunning coastline of Norway with Hurtigruten, the famous coastal voyage route that showcases the breathtaking beauty of this Nordic gem. Known as the world's most scenic sea voyage, Hurtigruten o ers an unforgettable experience for travellers seeking to immerse themselves in the rich history, art, and traditions of Norway.

For cultural enthusiasts, Hurtigruten is a treasure trove of Norwegian heritage. As you traverse the pristine waters, you will encounter charming coastal villages that have preserved their traditional way of life for centuries. From the bustling shing towns to the remote Arctic settlements, each stop along the route unveils a fascinating chapter of Norway's history. Immerse yourself in the local culture, taste traditional cuisine, and witness age-old traditions that have stood the test of time.

Nature lovers and Northern Lights enthusiasts will nd their dreams come true as they embark on this coastal voyage. Norway's dramatic landscapes unfold before your eyes, with majestic mountains, cascading waterfalls, and awe-inspiring fjords providing a captivating backdrop. As you sail through the Arctic Circle, be prepared to witness the ethereal dance of the Northern Lights illuminating the night sky. With specially designed tours and expert guides, Hurtigruten ensures you have the best chance of witnessing this mesmerizing phenomenon.

For those seeking vibrant city experiences,
Hurtigruten o        ers the perfect blend of coastal charm and urban exploration. Explore the vibrant cities of Oslo, Bergen, and Trondheim, each with its unique character and attractions. Discover the architectural wonders, immerse yourself in the vibrant arts scene, and indulge in the culinary delights that these cities have to o        er. With city-speci  c travel tips, Hurtigruten ensures you make the most of your time in each city, allowing you to create lasting memories.

Whether you are a cultural enthusiast, a Northern Lights chaser, or a city explorer, Hurtigruten's coastal voyage route along Norway's coast is the ultimate journey of discovery. Let the magic of Norway unfold before your eyes as you immerse yourself in its art, history, and traditions. Prepare to be captivated by the breathtaking landscapes, enchanted by the local culture, and awed by the natural wonders that make Norway a truly unique destination.

## The Polar Light Center in Tromsø for learning about the Northern Lights.

The Polar Light Center in Tromsø for learning about the Northern Lights

If you are fascinated by the ethereal beauty of the Northern Lights and eager to delve deeper into the science and mystique behind this natural phenomenon, then a visit to the Polar Light Center in Tromsø is an absolute must. Situated in the heart of Norway's Arctic region, Tromsø is known as one of the best places in the world to witness the mesmerizing dance of the Aurora Borealis. And at the Polar Light Center, you can not only witness the magic but also gain a comprehensive understanding of the Northern Lights.

For cultural travelers seeking to explore the rich history, art, and traditions of Norway, the Polar Light Center oers a unique opportunity to immerse oneself in the cultural signi cance of the Northern Lights. The center showcases an array of exhibits that delve into the folklore, myths, and legends surrounding this celestial spectacle. Learn about the ancient Sami people of

Norway and their spiritual connection to the lights, and discover how the Northern Lights have inspired artists and writers throughout history.

For those specializing in chasing the Northern Lights phenomenon, the Polar Light Center provides invaluable insights and practical tips. The center's knowledgeable sta , comprised of expert researchers and experienced guides, are there to assist you in planning your Northern Lights adventure. From understanding the best time and location to witness the lights to learning how to photograph them, the Polar Light Center equips you with the knowledge you need to make the most of your Northern Lights experience.

Even for city travelers exploring the vibrant cities of Oslo, Bergen, and Trondheim, a visit to the Polar Light Center is a worthwhile detour. The center oers city-specic travel tips, helping you plan your visit to Tromsø and ensuring that you don't miss out on this once-in-a-lifetime opportunity. Whether you choose to join a guided tour or explore independently, the

Polar Light Center is a fantastic resource to enhance your overall travel experience in Norway.

In conclusion, the Polar Light Center in Tromsø is an essential destination for travelers with a passion for the Northern Lights. It caters to the interests of cultural travelers, Northern Lights enthusiasts, and city explorers alike, o ering a comprehensive and enriching experience. Immerse yourself in the magic of the Aurora Borealis and gain a deeper understanding of this natural wonder at the Polar Light Center in Tromsø.

# Preikestolen, a stunning cliff with breathtaking views.

Preikestolen, a stunning cli with breathtaking views

As you journey through the enchanting landscapes of Norway, there is a place that is sure to leave you spellbound - Preikestolen, also known as the Pulpit Rock. Perched high above the Lysefjord, this majestic cli  o    ers awe-inspiring views that will take your breath away.

For the cultural travel guide to Norway, Preikestolen is a must-visit destination. Its history dates back thousands of years, and it has been a place of pilgrimage for centuries. The cli  was formed during the last ice age, and its distinct shape has captivated artists and writers throughout history. As you stand on the edge of Preikestolen, you can't help but feel the weight of centuries of human existence.

For the Northern Lights travel guide to Norway, Preikestolen o  ers a unique opportunity to witness the mesmerizing dance of colors in the night sky. Imagine standing on the cli   , surrounded by the ethereal glow of the Aurora Borealis as it illuminates the fjord below. It's a sight that will stay with you forever, a moment of pure magic.

For the city travel guide to Norway, Preikestolen is easily accessible from the vibrant cities of Oslo, Bergen, and Trondheim. You can embark on a day trip or spend a few nights in the nearby towns, immersing yourself in the local culture and traditions. From the cities, you can reach Preikestolen by a combination of train, bus, and ferry, making it a convenient addition to your itinerary.

But what truly sets Preikestolen apart is its natural beauty. The cli stands at 604 meters above sea level, o        ering panoramic views of the surrounding fjords and mountains. The ever-changing weather adds to the drama, with misty mornings and golden sunsets creating a magical atmosphere. Whether you're an avid hiker or simply enjoy breathtaking scenery, Preikestolen will leave you in awe.

So, fellow travelers, as you explore the rich history, art, and traditions of Norway, don't miss the opportunity to visit

Preikestolen. It is a place that encapsulates the very essence of this remarkable country - its rugged beauty, its ancient history, and its ability to inspire awe and wonder. Prepare to be amazed as you stand on the edge of Preikestolen, taking in the breathtaking views that stretch as far as the eye can see.

## Stave Churches, such as Urnes Stave Church.

# Stave Churches, such as Urnes Stave Church

Norway, a land of stunning landscapes and rich cultural heritage, is home to the unique and fascinating stave churches. These remarkable structures, dating back to the medieval times, are a testament to Norway's architectural prowess and religious history. Among them, the Urnes Stave Church stands out as a true gem, captivating travelers and history enthusiasts alike.

Stave churches are wooden structures characterized by their distinctive post-and-beam construction, with vertical staves supporting the walls and roof. This ancient building technique, prevalent in medieval Scandinavia, has allowed these churches to withstand the test of time, enduring for centuries while preserving their original beauty.

Urnes Stave Church, located in the idyllic Sognefjord region, is a UNESCO World Heritage site and the oldest stave church in Norway. Dating back to the 12th century, this architectural masterpiece is a prime example of the country's rich history and artistic traditions. Its intricate carvings, depicting scenes from Norse mythology and Christian symbolism, are a testament to the craftsmanship of the Viking age.

For cultural travelers seeking to explore the art and history of Norway, a visit to Urnes Stave Church is an absolute must. Stepping inside this enchanting wooden sanctuary, travelers are transported back in time, immersing themselves in the country's medieval past. The dimly lit interior, adorned with ornate wood carvings and delicate paintings, creates an atmosphere of mystique and reverence.

Moreover, for those fascinated by the Northern Lights phenomenon, a trip to Urnes Stave Church o ers a unique opportunity to witness this celestial spectacle against the backdrop of a historical marvel. Imagine standing amidst the ancient wooden beams, gazing up at the dancing lights in the night sky – a moment of pure magic and wonder.

While exploring the vibrant cities of Oslo, Bergen, and Trondheim, don't miss the chance to venture into the Norwegian countryside and discover the hidden treasures of the stave churches. These architectural wonders are not only a testament to Norway's rich cultural heritage but also a gateway to a bygone era, where history, art, and traditions seamlessly merge.

In conclusion, stave churches, with Urnes Stave Church as a prime example, o er travelers a unique opportunity to delve into Norway's rich history, art, and traditions. Whether you are a cultural enthusiast, a Northern Lights chaser, or a city explorer, a visit to these remarkable wooden structures is sure to leave you captivated and inspired. Embark on a journey through time and immerse yourself in the magic of Norway's stave churches.

# The North Cape, the northernmost point of Europe.

The North Cape, the northernmost point of Europe, is a destination that truly captures the essence of Norway's natural beauty and rugged charm. Situated on the island of Magerøya in the Arctic Ocean, this iconic landmark has long been a magnet for adventurers and nature enthusiasts alike.

For the cultural travel guide to Norway, the North Cape o ers a unique opportunity to delve into the country's rich history. Standing on the edge of the cli , travelers can imagine the Vikings who once navigated these treacherous waters, or the indigenous Sami people who have called this region home for centuries. The North Cape Visitor Centre provides a fascinating insight into the cultural heritage of the area, with exhibits that showcase the traditions, folklore, and way of life of the people who have lived in this remote corner of Europe.

For those chasing the mesmerizing Northern Lights phenomenon, the North Cape is an ideal location to witness this awe-inspiring natural spectacle. With its remote location and minimal light pollution, the chances of encountering the dancing colors of the Aurora Borealis are greatly increased. Imagine standing on the North Cape, gazing up at the night sky as vibrant hues of green, purple, and blue swirl above you - it is an experience that will stay with you forever.

Even for city travelers, a visit to the North Cape is a must. While Oslo, Bergen, and Trondheim o er vibrant city life, the North Cape provides a stark contrast with its untamed wilderness. It is a place of solitude and tranquility, where one can escape the hustle and bustle of urban living and reconnect with nature. The journey to the North Cape is an adventure in itself, with breathtaking landscapes, fjords, and scenic routes that will leave you in awe at every turn.

In conclusion, the North Cape is a destination that appeals to a wide range of travelers. Whether you are a cultural enthusiast, a Northern Lights chaser, or a city explorer, this northernmost point of Europe o ers a unique and unforgettable experience. From its rich history and cultural heritage to its mesmerizing natural wonders, the North Cape truly embodies the magic of Norway.

## The Northern Lights in Northern Norway, especially in Tromsø.

The Northern Lights in Northern Norway, especially in Tromsø

As the night falls over the Arctic Circle, a mystical phenomenon lights up the sky, captivating the hearts of all who witness it. The Northern Lights, also known as the Aurora Borealis, is a breathtaking display of vibrant colors dancing across the heavens. Nowhere is this ethereal spectacle more dazzling than in Northern Norway, and particularly in the enchanting city of Tromsø.

Tromsø, nestled amidst snow-capped mountains and surrounded by fjords, is often referred to as the "Gateway to the Arctic." Its unique geographical location, with its proximity to the North Pole, makes it one of the best places on Earth to witness the Northern Lights. Travellers ock to this picturesque city from all corners of the globe, hoping to catch a glimpse of this natural wonder.

The magic of the Northern Lights lies in its unpredictability. They appear when solar particles collide with the Earth's atmosphere, creating a mesmerizing display of colors, ranging from vibrant greens and blues to subtle pinks and purples. The best time to see the Northern Lights in Tromsø is from September to April, when the nights are long and the sky is dark.

To enhance your chances of witnessing this celestial spectacle, it is advisable to join a guided tour. Experienced guides, well-versed in the science and folklore surrounding the Northern Lights, will take you to the best viewing spots, away from light pollution. They will regale you with captivating stories and myths associated with the lights, adding a touch of magic to your experience.

Apart from the Northern Lights, Tromsø o    ers a plethora of cultural and historical attractions. The city is home to the iconic Arctic Cathedral, a masterpiece of modern architecture, with its towering triangular shape and stunning stained glass windows. The Polar Museum provides insight into the region's rich history of polar exploration, while the Sami Museum o      ers a glimpse into the indigenous culture of the Sami people.

Tromsø's vibrant city life is also worth exploring. Its lively cafes, restaurants, and bars provide the perfect backdrop for mingling with locals and immersing yourself in the city's vibrant atmosphere. Don't forget to sample the local delicacies, such as reindeer meat and freshly caught Arctic seafood.

In conclusion, a journey to Tromsø in Northern Norway is an opportunity to witness the aweinspiring Northern Lights and delve into the rich cultural heritage of this Arctic region. Whether you are a cultural enthusiast, a Northern Lights chaser, or a city explorer, Tromsø promises an unforgettable experience that will leave you in awe of the magic of Norway.

# The city of Bergen with its historic harbor district, Bryggen.

The city of Bergen with its historic harbor district,

Bryggen

Nestled amidst Norway's stunning landscape lies the enchanting city of Bergen, a place where history comes alive and cultural treasures abound. At the heart of this vibrant city is the historic harbor district known as Bryggen, a UNESCO World Heritage site that beckons travelers with its timeless charm.

As you wander through the narrow, cobbled streets of Bryggen, you can't help but be transported back in time. The iconic wooden buildings, dating back to the 14th century, stand tall and proud, o    ering a glimpse into Bergen's rich Hanseatic past. These structures, once bustling with merchants and trade, now house a myriad of shops, cafes, and museums, each o    ering a unique perspective on the city's history and traditions.

One of the must-visit attractions in Bryggen is the Hanseatic Museum and Schøtstuene, which provides a fascinating insight into the lives of the Hanseatic merchants who once called this place home. Step inside the preserved wooden buildings and explore the recreated living quarters, workshops, and o ces, immersing yourself in the daily life of these medieval traders.

Another highlight of Bryggen is the Bergenhus Fortress, a monumental structure that has guarded the city for centuries. Explore its ancient halls, visit the Rosenkrantz Tower, and marvel at the stunning views of the harbor from the top. The fortress also houses the Håkon's Hall, a grand medieval banquet hall that hosts concerts and events, adding a touch of magic to your visit.

For art enthusiasts, the KODE Art Museums of Bergen o er a treasure trove of works by renowned Norwegian artists such as Edvard Munch and Nikolai Astrup. From contemporary art to classical paintings, these museums provide a comprehensive overview of Norway's artistic heritage and are a must-visit for any cultural traveler.

As you venture further into Bryggen, allow yourself to get lost in its labyrinthine alleys, discovering hidden gems at every turn.

Explore the local craft shops, where artisans showcase their traditional skills, creating intricate woodwork, jewelry, and textiles. Don't forget to sample the local cuisine, with seafood being a particular specialty. Indulge in freshly caught sh, mouthwatering shrimp, and the famous Bergen sh soup, a culinary delight that will leave you craving for more.

Whether you are a cultural explorer, a Northern Lights enthusiast, or a city lover, the city of Bergen and its historic harbor district, Bryggen, will captivate your senses and leave an indelible mark on your journey through Norway. Immerse yourself in its rich history, admire its artistic treasures, and let the magic of this enchanting city unfold before your eyes.

# The Fjords of Norway, including Geirangerfjord and Nærøyfjord.

The Fjords of Norway, including Geirangerfjord and Nærøyfjord

Norway is renowned for its breathtaking natural beauty, and the fjords are undoubtedly one of its most iconic features. These dramatic, steep-sided valleys carved by ancient glaciers o er a truly magical and awe-inspiring experience. In this subchapter, we will delve into two of the most famous fjords in Norway: Geirangerfjord and Nærøyfjord.

Geirangerfjord, a UNESCO World Heritage site, is often called the crown jewel of the Norwegian fjords. Located in the western part of the country, it stretches for 15 kilometers and is surrounded by towering mountains and cascading waterfalls. The fjord is best explored by taking a scenic cruise, allowing you to witness the sheer grandeur of the landscape. As you sail through the crystal-clear waters, you will be captivated by the immensity of the cli s and the beauty of the Seven Sisters and the Bridal Veil waterfalls.

Nærøyfjord, another UNESCO World Heritage site, is located in the western part of Norway and is considered one of the narrowest fjords in Europe. This 17-kilometer long fjord is known for its dramatic landscapes, with steep mountainsides plunging into the deep blue waters below. A popular way to experience Nærøyfjord is by taking a scenic train journey on the Flåm Railway, which o ers breathtaking views as it winds its way through the rugged terrain. You can also explore the fjord by kayak or take a leisurely hike along its shores, immersing yourself in the tranquility and beauty of the surrounding nature.

For cultural enthusiasts, these fjords hold a wealth of history and traditions. The small villages along the fjords o er a glimpse into the traditional Norwegian way of life, with charming wooden houses and picturesque farmsteads dotting the landscape. You can visit the historic stave churches, such as the one in Urnes, which dates back to the 12th century and is considered a masterpiece of medieval wooden architecture.

For those seeking the mesmerizing Northern Lights phenomenon, the fjords provide a unique setting. The dark, clear skies and the re ection of the lights on the calm waters create a surreal and unforgettable experience. Imagine witnessing the

dancing colors of the Aurora Borealis amidst the majestic fjords –
a truly magical moment.

Whether you are a cultural traveler, a Northern Lights enthusiast,
or simply someone looking to explore the vibrant cities of
Norway, the fjords, especially Geirangerfjord and Nærøyfjord,
are a must-visit destination. Immerse yourself in the awe-
inspiring beauty, rich history, and traditions that Norway has to o
er, and let the magic of the fjords leave an indelible mark on your
journey.

# Norway food

## Brunost - Brown Cheese

Brunost, also known as brown cheese, is a unique Norwegian
delicacy that has been enjoyed for centuries. This distinct cheese
is made from the whey, or liquid, that is left over from the
production of other cheeses. The whey is cooked until it

caramelizes, giving the cheese its signature brown color and sweet, caramel-like avor.

For travellers visiting Norway, trying brunost is a must-do experience. It is not only a delicious treat but also a cultural symbol of Norwegian cuisine. The cheese is often served as a topping on bread or crackers and can be enjoyed with a variety of accompaniments such as jam, honey, or fresh fruit.

Cultural travel guide Norway

Exploring the rich history, art, and traditions of Norway is incomplete without indulging in the local culinary delights. Brunost represents the essence of Norwegian food culture, re ecting the resourcefulness and creativity of the Norwegian people. Its unique production process and distinct taste make it a fascinating part of Norway's gastronomic heritage.

Northern Lights travel guide Norway

While chasing the mesmerizing Northern Lights phenomenon in Norway, travellers can take a break and warm themselves up with a taste of brunost. The rich, creamy texture and sweet avor of this cheese provide a comforting and satisfying experience. It is the perfect treat to enjoy while waiting for the majestic auroras to light up the night sky.

City travel guide Norway

As travellers explore the vibrant cities of Oslo, Bergen, and Trondheim, they can also discover the culinary delights of brunost. This cheese is readily available in local markets, specialty shops, and even some restaurants and cafes. It can be purchased in various forms, including slices, cubes, or even spreadable versions. Tasting brunost gives travellers a unique opportunity to experience the authentic avors of Norway's cities.

In conclusion, brunost, or brown cheese, is a delicious and culturally signi    cant delicacy in Norway. Whether you are a cultural enthusiast, a Northern Lights chaser, or a city explorer, trying brunost is an essential part of your Norwegian journey. So, don't miss the chance to indulge in this sweet and savory treat and discover the magic of Norway's culinary traditions.

## Kjøttkaker - Meatballs

When it comes to Norwegian cuisine, one dish that stands out as a classic comfort food is kjøttkaker, also known as meatballs. These avorful, tender morsels are a staple in Norwegian households and can be found on menus throughout the country. In this subchapter, we delve into the history, preparation, and cultural signi cance of this beloved dish.

The origins of kjøttkaker can be traced back to the time of the Vikings, who were known for their hearty and robust meals. Over the centuries, the recipe has evolved, but the essence remains the same - a delicious blend of ground meat, breadcrumbs, onions, and spices.

Traditionally, kjøttkaker were made using a combination of beef and pork, resulting in a rich and savory avor. However, variations using reindeer, lamb, or even sh can also be found in di   erent regions of Norway. Each variation adds its own unique twist to the dish, re   ecting the diverse culinary traditions of the country.

The preparation of kjøttkaker is an art form in itself. The mixture is carefully seasoned with salt, pepper, and nutmeg, before being formed into small, round patties. These patties are then fried to perfection, creating a crispy exterior while maintaining a juicy interior. The meatballs are typically served with creamy mashed potatoes, lingonberry sauce, and a side of vegetables.

In Norwegian culture, kjøttkaker holds a special place. It is often served during festive occasions and family gatherings, bringing people together over a delicious meal. The dish also represents the appreciation of nature's bounty, as the ingredients used in kjøttkaker are often sourced locally.

For travelers visiting Norway, trying kjøttkaker is a must. Many traditional restaurants and cafes o   er this iconic dish, providing a taste of authentic Norwegian cuisine. Whether you are a cultural traveler exploring the rich history and traditions of Norway, a Northern Lights enthusiast mesmerized by the country's natural wonders, or a city explorer in search of vibrant culinary experiences, kjøttkaker is a delightful addition to your gastronomic journey.

So, next time you nd yourself in Norway, don't miss the opportunity to savor the magic of kjøttkaker. It's a dish that encapsulates the heart and soul of
Norwegian cuisine, bringing together avors, history, and traditions in each delectable bite.

## Raspeballer - Potato Dumplings

For the curious traveler seeking to explore the rich culinary traditions of Norway, Raspeballer, also known as potato dumplings, is a dish that should not be missed. This hearty and delicious meal has a long history in Norwegian cuisine and is a staple in many households and restaurants throughout the country.

Raspeballer is a simple yet satisfying dish made primarily from potatoes, our, and salt. The dough is formed into balls, boiled until cooked through, and then served with a variety of accompaniments. Traditionally, these dumplings are enjoyed with salted meats such as bacon or cured ham, along with a side of cooked carrots, rutabagas, and lingonberry jam. The combination of avors and textures creates a truly delightful dining experience.

While Raspeballer may seem like a humble dish, its origins date back centuries. Historically, it was a popular meal among farmers and shermen who needed a lling and nutritious meal to sustain them during long days of work. Over time, it has become a beloved comfort food, cherished by Norwegians and visitors alike.

For the cultural traveler, sampling Raspeballer o    ers a unique glimpse into the country's culinary heritage. Each region of

Norway has its own variation of this dish, with slight di erences in ingredients and preparation methods. Exploring the diverse avors and techniques of Raspeballer across the country is a journey in itself, allowing one to appreciate the rich cultural tapestry that de nes Norway.

For those embarking on a Northern Lights adventure, indulging in Raspeballer is the perfect way to warm up after a thrilling night of chasing the mesmerizing aurora borealis. Its hearty and lling nature provides the sustenance needed to brave the cold winter nights, while its comforting avors o er a taste of Norwegian hospitality.

Even for those exploring the vibrant cities of Oslo, Bergen, and Trondheim, Raspeballer can be found in local restaurants and markets. City travelers can immerse themselves in the culinary delights of Norway by sampling this traditional dish, gaining a deeper understanding of the country's culture and traditions. In conclusion, Raspeballer is a culinary treasure that encapsulates the magic of Norway. Its humble origins, diverse regional variations, and comforting avors make it a must-try dish for any traveler seeking to delve into the cultural, historical, and artistic wonders of this beautiful country. Whether you're a cultural enthusiast, a Northern Lights chaser, or a city explorer, Raspeballer promises to delight your taste buds and leave a lasting impression of your journey through Norway.

## Fårikål - Mutton and Cabbage Stew

Norway is a land of rich culinary traditions, and one dish that stands out as a true symbol of Norwegian comfort food is Fårikål. This hearty mutton and cabbage stew has been a staple of Norwegian cuisine for centuries, and its simplicity and deliciousness have made it a favorite among locals and visitors alike.

Fårikål, which translates to "sheep in cabbage," is a dish that perfectly encapsulates the essence of Norwegian cuisine. It consists of tender mutton, usually from the shoulder or leg, simmered slowly with cabbage, whole black peppercorns, and a touch of salt. The result is a avorful and comforting stew that warms both body and soul.

The origins of Fårikål can be traced back to the rural areas of Norway, where sheep farming was a common practice. In the autumn, when the sheep were ready for slaughter, the tradition of making Fårikål began. The dish was a way to preserve the meat for the long, cold winter months ahead. The combination of mutton and cabbage, along with the slow cooking process, allowed for the avors to meld together, creating a dish that could be enjoyed throughout the winter.

Today, Fårikål is still a beloved dish in Norway, and it holds a special place in Norwegian culture. In fact, it has even been designated as the national dish of Norway, a testament to its popularity and signi      cance. Every year on the last Thursday of September, Norwegians come together to celebrate Fårikålens Festdag (Fårikål Day), where friends and family gather to enjoy a steaming bowl of this delicious stew.

For travelers visiting Norway, trying Fårikål is a must. Whether you are exploring the rich history, art, and traditions of the country, chasing the mesmerizing Northern Lights, or exploring the vibrant cities of Oslo, Bergen, and Trondheim, Fårikål provides a taste of authentic Norwegian cuisine.

In cities like Oslo and Bergen, you can nd Fårikål on the menus of traditional Norwegian restaurants, where it is often served with boiled potatoes and lingonberry sauce. For those venturing into the countryside, visiting a farm or attending a local festival may o er the opportunity to taste Fårikål made in the traditional way.

No matter where you try Fårikål, the experience of savoring this iconic Norwegian dish will undoubtedly leave you with a deeper appreciation for the country's culinary heritage. So, don't miss the chance to indulge in the magic of Fårikål during your journey through Norway.

# Rak sk - Fermented Fish

Norway is a land of fascinating traditions, and one that stands out in particular is the practice of fermenting sh to create a unique delicacy called rak sk. A staple in Norwegian cuisine for centuries, rak      sk holds a special place in the hearts and taste buds of the locals. For travellers seeking a true cultural experience, delving into the world of rak      sk is a must.

Rak     sk is typically made from freshwater sh, such as trout or char, that are caught during the autumn months when they are at their prime. The sh are carefully cleaned and gutted, then salted and left to ferment for several weeks. This ancient preservation method allows the sh to develop a distinct, pungent avor and a soft, tender texture.

The process of making rak      sk is not for the faint of heart, but the end result is worth the eort. Travellers who dare to try this traditional dish will be rewarded with a truly unique culinary experience. The strong aroma and intense taste may be an acquired taste for some, but for those who appreciate bold flavors, rakfisk is a delight.

To fully appreciate rakfisk, it is best to enjoy it the way the Norwegians do. Head to a local market or festival where you can sample different varieties of rakfisk, paired with traditional accompaniments such as flatbread, sour cream, onions, and potatoes. The combination of flavors and textures is a true taste of Norway's rich culinary heritage.

For the adventurous travellers who are looking to take their rakfisk experience to the next level, there are even rakfisk tasting tours available. These tours take you on a journey through the heartland of rakfisk production, where you can visit traditional fish farms and learn about the history and techniques behind this age-old tradition. It is a chance to immerse yourself in the local culture and gain a deeper understanding of Norway's culinary traditions.

Whether you are a cultural enthusiast, a Northern Lights chaser, or a city explorer, rakfisk is an essential part of the

Norwegian experience. It is a taste of history, art, and traditions all in one bite. So, don't miss the opportunity to embark on this gastronomic adventure and discover the magic of rak      sk in Norway.

## Gravlaks - Gravlax (Cured Salmon)

Norway is known for its stunning landscapes, picturesque fjords, and vibrant cities, but it also boasts a rich culinary heritage. One dish that encapsulates the essence of Norwegian cuisine is gravlaks, or gravlax, a traditional cured salmon dish that has been a staple in Norwegian culture for centuries.

Gravlaks is a true delicacy that combines simplicity with exquisite avors. The name "gravlaks" literally translates to "buried salmon," as the traditional method of curing involved burying the sh in the sand to ferment. Today, the curing process has evolved, but the dish has retained its traditional avors and techniques.

To make gravlaks, a fresh salmon llet is coated in a mixture of salt, sugar, and dill and left to cure for a few days. The salt draws out the moisture from the sh, creating a rm and slightly salty texture, while the sugar and dill infuse it with a delicate sweetness and herbal aroma. The result is a tender, melt-in-your-mouth salmon that is bursting with avor.

Gravlaks is typically served thinly sliced, often on rye bread with a mustard-dill sauce called "sennepssaus." The combination of the salty salmon, tangy sauce, and earthy rye bread creates a symphony of avors that is sure to delight your taste buds.

For cultural travelers, trying gravlaks is a must-do when visiting Norway. It not only o ers a taste of the country's culinary traditions but also provides a glimpse into its history and heritage. Gravlaks has been enjoyed in Norway since the medieval times, and it continues to be a beloved dish today, often served on special occasions and holidays.

Northern Lights enthusiasts will also nd gravlaks to be a delightful addition to their culinary adventures. After a long day of chasing the mesmerizing aurora borealis, indulging in a plate of gravlaks is the perfect way to warm up and savor the avors of Norway.

Even city travelers can experience the magic of gravlaks. Many restaurants in Oslo, Bergen, and Trondheim o er this traditional dish on their menus, allowing visitors to explore the vibrant cities while also immersing themselves in the country's culinary traditions.

Whether you are a cultural traveler, a Northern Lights enthusiast, or a city explorer, don't miss the opportunity to try gravlaks during your visit to Norway. It is a culinary masterpiece that truly captures the magic of this beautiful country.

# Pølse med Lompe - Hot Dog with Potato Pancake

When it comes to traditional Norwegian street food, Pølse med Lompe is an absolute must-try. This delicious dish combines the simplicity of a hot dog with the unique twist of a potato pancake, creating a mouthwatering treat that will leave your taste buds begging for more.

Pølse med Lompe is a popular snack found throughout Norway, enjoyed by locals and visitors alike. It is a prime example of how Norway combines its culinary traditions with modern in uences, creating a fusion of avors that is both familiar and unique.

The star of this dish is the Pølse, a Norwegian sausage made from a blend of pork, beef, and spices. These sausages are grilled to perfection, giving them a slightly smoky and savory avor that pairs perfectly with the other ingredients.

The Lompe, on the other hand, is a thin potato pancake that acts as the bun for the hot dog. Made from grated potatoes, our, and salt, the Lompe is cooked until golden brown and crispy on the outside while remaining soft and tender on the inside. It adds a delightful texture to the dish and enhances the overall taste experience.

To assemble your Pølse med Lompe, start by placing the grilled sausage on top of the Lompe. Then, add your choice of toppings. Traditional options include ketchup, mustard, and crispy fried onions. However, you can also get creative and add pickles, sauerkraut, or even cheese to make it your own.

The great thing about Pølse med Lompe is that it can be enjoyed anywhere, making it the perfect on-thego snack for travelers exploring Norway's vibrant cities. Whether you're strolling through the streets of Oslo, Bergen, or Trondheim, you're bound to nd a food stand or food truck serving up this delectable treat.

So, the next time you nd yourself in Norway, don't miss the opportunity to indulge in the magic of Pølse med Lompe. It's a true taste of Norwegian culture, combining history, art, and tradition into one delicious bite.

## Koldtbord - Cold Buffet

In the land of breathtaking landscapes and rich cultural heritage, Norway o    ers not only stunning natural wonders but also a delightful culinary experience. One traditional Norwegian dining concept that stands out is the Koldtbord, or the Cold Bu    et. This subchapter will take you on a gastronomic journey through the unique and mouthwatering dishes served on a Koldtbord, as well as the cultural signi    cance behind this culinary tradition.

The Koldtbord is a quintessential part of Norwegian cuisine, often served during festive occasions, family gatherings, and celebrations. It is a lavish spread of cold dishes, carefully arranged to showcase the best of Norway's culinary traditions. From smoked salmon to cured meats, pickled herring to marinated vegetables, the Koldtbord o ers an array of avors and textures that will leave you craving for more.

One of the highlights of a Koldtbord is the variety of seafood dishes. Norway's coastal landscape provides an abundance of fresh seafood, and it is beautifully represented on the cold bu et. Delicacies like gravlaks (cured salmon), rak      sk (fermented sh), and shrimp salad are sure to tantalize your taste buds. Don't forget to try the traditional lute   sk, a dried and rehydrated cod dish, which is often considered a delicacy during Christmas time.

The Koldtbord is not just about the food, but also about the cultural signi cance it holds. It is a re    ection of Norwegian society's emphasis on togetherness, generosity, and the celebration of food. Gathering around a table lled with delicious dishes is a way for Norwegians to connect, share stories, and strengthen family and community bonds.

For the cultural travel guide to Norway, exploring the Koldtbord is an essential part of understanding the country's culinary traditions. It allows you to delve deeper into the cultural signi cance of food in Norwegian society and discover the stories behind each dish.

If you are a Northern Lights enthusiast, the Koldtbord can be a perfect way to warm up after a mesmerizing night of chasing the aurora borealis. The cozy atmosphere, traditional dishes, and the company of fellow travelers will create an unforgettable experience.

Even if you are a city traveler, exploring the vibrant cities of Oslo, Bergen, or Trondheim, a Koldtbord experience can be a great way to immerse yourself in the local food scene. Many restaurants and cafes in these cities o er their own version of the Cold Bu et, combining traditional Norwegian avors with a modern twist.

Whether you are a cultural explorer, a Northern Lights chaser, or a city enthusiast, the Koldtbord is a culinary adventure that should not be missed. So, sit back, indulge in the avors of

Norway, and let the

Koldtbord take you on a journey through art, history, and

traditions.

## Lute sk - Lute sk (Stock sh soaked in lye)

Lute   sk, a traditional Norwegian dish, holds a special place in

the hearts and stomachs of locals. This unique delicacy, made

from stock   sh soaked in lye, is a testament to Norway's rich

culinary heritage. For travellers seeking an authentic cultural

experience, lute    sk is a must-try dish that embodies the

traditions and avors of this beautiful country.

The process of making lute        sk is an age-old tradition that

dates back centuries. It begins with stock      sh, which is dried,

salted cod that has been air-dried on wooden racks. This stock

sh is then soaked in a water and lye solution for several days,

resulting in a gelatinous texture. The sh is then rinsed and

cooked, often served with boiled potatoes, peas, bacon, and a

generous amount of melted butter.

For cultural enthusiasts, lute    sk o    ers a unique insight into Norway's history and culinary customs. The dish has deep roots in the country's Viking past, where preserving sh through drying and salting was a necessity for survival in the harsh Nordic climate. Over time, this preservation method evolved into the beloved tradition of lute   sk.

Travellers with a passion for art and history will nd lute    sk to be a delicious link to Norway's past. This dish has been celebrated in Norwegian literature, music, and art as a symbol of cultural identity. It has inspired countless poems and stories, becoming a beloved icon in the Norwegian cultural landscape.

For those in pursuit of the mesmerizing Northern Lights phenomenon, indulging in lute sk is a delightful way to immerse oneself in the local traditions while chasing the aurora borealis. Many cosy restaurants and lodges in Northern Norway o er lute sk as a specialty, allowing visitors to experience the magic of the Northern Lights and the magic of lute sk simultaneously.

Even in the vibrant cities of Oslo, Bergen, and Trondheim, lute sk can be found in traditional restaurants and markets, allowing city explorers to taste the quintessential  avors of Norway. From quaint  sh markets to lively city festivals, lute sk is a beloved dish that unites locals and visitors alike in celebration of Norwegian culture and cuisine.

Whether you are a cultural enthusiast, a Northern Lights chaser, or a city explorer, lute sk is an essential part of any journey to Norway. It is a culinary adventure that invites travellers to immerse themselves in the rich history, art, and traditions of this enchanting country. So, don't miss the opportunity to try lute sk and savor the magic of Norway on your next adventure.

Raspeballer - Potato Dumplings

Norway is a country that prides itself on its rich culinary traditions, and one dish that holds a special place in the hearts of Norwegians is raspeballer, also known as potato dumplings. These hearty dumplings have been a staple in Norwegian cuisine for centuries and continue to be a beloved comfort food to this day.

Raspeballer are made by mixing grated potatoes with our, salt, and sometimes a bit of butter. The mixture is then shaped into small balls and boiled until they are tender and u y. Traditionally, they are served with boiled salted pork, bacon, or sausages, along with melted butter and a generous helping of lingonberry jam.

For travelers seeking to explore the cultural and culinary traditions of Norway, trying raspeballer is a must. This dish not only showcases the simple yet delicious avors of Norwegian cuisine but also provides a glimpse into the country's history and rural traditions.

In Northern Norway, where the winters are long and cold, raspeballer has been a popular dish among shermen and farmers for centuries. The dumplings were easy to prepare, using simple ingredients that were readily available. They provided a lling and nutritious meal that would keep them energized during long days of work.

In recent years, raspeballer has gained popularity beyond rural areas and can now be found in many Norwegian cities as well. In fact, several restaurants in Oslo, Bergen, and Trondheim have put their own modern twist on this traditional dish, o ering unique variations and avor combinations.

For those travelers interested in chasing the mesmerizing Northern Lights phenomenon in
Norway, enjoying a warm plate of raspeballer after a long day of hunting the aurora borealis is the perfect way to end the night. The hearty dumplings provide much-needed warmth and sustenance, while the lingonberry jam adds a touch of sweetness to balance the avors.

Whether you're a cultural enthusiast, a Northern Lights chaser, or a city explorer, don't miss the opportunity to savor the traditional avors of Norway with a plate of raspeballer. This humble dish embodies the true essence of Norwegian cuisine and will leave you craving for more. So, grab a fork and experience the magic of raspeballer for yourself. Skål!

## Practical Information for Travelers

### Essential travel tips for visiting Norway

Norway is a country of breathtaking natural beauty, rich history, and vibrant culture. Whether you are an avid cultural explorer, a Northern Lights enthusiast, or a city lover, this chapter aims to provide you with essential travel tips to make the most of your visit to this enchanting country.

For the cultural travel guide Norway, exploring the rich history, art, and traditions of Norway, it is important to plan your itinerary accordingly. Start your journey in Oslo, the capital city, where you can visit iconic museums like the Viking Ship Museum and the Oslo Opera House. Don't miss the chance to explore the charming city of Bergen, with its UNESCO-listed Bryggen Wharf and the nearby Edvard Grieg's Troldhaugen. To truly immerse yourself in Norwegian traditions, make sure to attend a traditional folk music or dance performance and try some authentic local dishes like lute sk or rak sk.

Northern Lights travel guide Norway enthusiasts will be awe-inspired by the magical phenomenon of the Aurora Borealis. The best time to witness this natural wonder is between September and March, and the most popular destinations for chasing the Northern Lights are Tromsø, Lofoten Islands, and Svalbard. Remember to dress warmly, bring a tripod for your camera, and be patient as the lights can be elusive. Additionally, consider joining a guided tour or hiring a local expert to increase your chances of spotting this mesmerizing spectacle.

City travel guide Norway focuses on exploring the vibrant cities of Oslo, Bergen, and Trondheim. In Oslo, take advantage of the e cient public transportation system, including trams, buses, and ferries, to navigate the city. Visit the Royal Palace, the Akershus Fortress, and take a stroll along the picturesque Aker Brygge waterfront. In Bergen, ride the Fløibanen funicular to enjoy panoramic views of the city, explore the historic Hanseatic Wharf, and wander through the colorful wooden houses of the Bryggen district. Lastly, in Trondheim, don't miss the imposing Nidaros Cathedral and the charming Old Town with its quaint wooden houses.

No matter which niche you belong to, it is essential to pack appropriate clothing for Norway's unpredictable weather. Layering is key, as temperatures can vary throughout the day. A waterproof jacket, sturdy walking shoes, and a warm hat and gloves are essential items to include in your suitcase.

In conclusion, Norway o ers a wealth of experiences for cultural enthusiasts, Northern Lights chasers, and city explorers alike. By following these essential travel tips, you will be well-prepared to embark on your journey through the magic of Norway.

## Transportation options within Norway

Norway, with its stunning landscapes, rich history, and vibrant cities, o ers a plethora of transportation options for travelers to explore and experience the magic of this Nordic country. Whether you are a cultural enthusiast, a Northern Lights chaser, or a city explorer, Norway has something for everyone.

For cultural travelers, Norway's transportation network is well-developed, making it easy to navigate between cities and towns. The country boasts an extensive rail network, connecting major cities such as Oslo, Bergen, and Trondheim. The trains o er comfortable and scenic journeys, allowing you to admire the breathtaking landscapes that Norway is famous for. Additionally, buses are a popular mode of transportation, especially for reaching more remote areas and smaller towns. They provide a convenient and a ordable way to explore the cultural heritage of Norway.

If you are a Northern Lights enthusiast, traveling to Norway's northern regions is a must. Transportation options in these areas are well-suited for Northern Lights chasing. Tromsø, known as the gateway to the Arctic, is a popular destination for witnessing this mesmerizing natural phenomenon. Flights are readily available from major cities to Tromsø, ensuring easy access to this magical location. Once there, local buses and taxis can be used to reach prime Northern Lights viewing spots and explore the surrounding areas.

For city travelers, Norway's vibrant cities o er a range of transportation options to make your exploration seamless. Oslo, the capital city, boasts an e cient public transportation system, including buses, trams, and metro trains. This allows you to e ortlessly navigate the city's cultural attractions, such as the Viking Ship Museum and the National Gallery. Bergen, known for its picturesque waterfront and colorful wooden houses, can be easily explored on foot or by using the city's light rail system. Trondheim, with its medieval architecture and vibrant student atmosphere, o ers a comprehensive bus network, making it easy to explore the city's rich history.

In conclusion, Norway provides a variety of transportation options for travelers of all interests. From the well-connected rail network for cultural travelers to the easy access ights for Northern Lights enthusiasts, and the e cient public transportation systems in the vibrant cities, Norway ensures that transportation is never a barrier to experiencing its art, history, and traditions. So, pack your bags, embark on an adventure, and let Norway's transportation options take you on a magical journey through this captivating country.

## Accommodation options in Norway

When planning your trip to Norway, one of the most important considerations is where to stay. Norway o ers a wide range of accommodation options to suit every traveler's preferences and budget. Whether you are a cultural enthusiast, a Northern Lights chaser, or simply looking to explore the vibrant cities of Oslo, Bergen, and Trondheim, there is something for everyone. For cultural travelers seeking an immersive experience, Norway o ers a unique opportunity to stay in traditional wooden cabins, known as "hytter." These cozy cabins are scattered throughout the countryside and provide a rustic yet comfortable accommodation option. Surrounded by breathtaking landscapes, they oer a true taste of Norwegian culture and allow you to connect with nature. Many hytter are equipped with basic amenities such as kitchenettes and private bathrooms, giving you the freedom to cook your own meals and enjoy the tranquil surroundings.

For those embarking on a Northern Lights adventure, consider staying in Tromsø, known as the gateway to the Arctic. This vibrant city o     ers a range of accommodations, from modern hotels to charming guesthouses. Some hotels even provide Northern Lights wake-up calls, ensuring you never miss out on this mesmerizing phenomenon. Additionally, Tromsø is home to several tour operators specializing in Northern Lights excursions, making it convenient for travelers to chase the aurora borealis.

If you are more inclined towards city exploration, Norway's major cities have a plethora of accommodation options to choose from. In Oslo, you can  nd luxury hotels with stunning views of the fjords, as well as budget-friendly hostels for backpackers. Bergen, famous for its UNESCO-listed Bryggen Wharf, o  ers a range of boutique hotels and guesthouses, allowing you to immerse yourself in the city's rich maritime history. Trondheim, with its charming cobblestone streets and medieval architecture, also o  ers a variety of accommodations, including centrally located hotels and cozy bed and breakfasts.

No matter which accommodation option you choose, it is important to book in advance, especially during the peak travel seasons. Norway's popularity as a tourist destination has been steadily increasing, and securing your preferred accommodation well in advance ensures a stress-free trip. Additionally, consider the location of your accommodation in relation to the attractions you wish to visit. Norway has an e cient public transportation system, but staying in close proximity to your desired sights can save you time and enhance your overall experience.

In conclusion, Norway o ers a diverse range of accommodation options to cater to the needs of cultural travelers, Northern Lights enthusiasts, and city explorers. From traditional hytter to modern hotels, there is something to suit every taste and budget. So, start planning your Norwegian adventure and make your stay in this magical country truly unforgettable.

## Norwegian cuisine and dining recommendations

Norway, known for its breathtaking landscapes and rich cultural heritage, also boasts a unique and diverse culinary scene. From fresh seafood to traditional delicacies, Norwegian cuisine o ers a delightful gastronomic experience for travelers exploring this beautiful country. In this subchapter, we will dive into the fascinating world of Norwegian cuisine and provide some dining recommendations for those seeking an authentic taste of Norway.

Seafood lovers will be in heaven in Norway, as the country is surrounded by the cold, clear waters of the North Atlantic and the Arctic Ocean. From succulent salmon to delicate cod and avorful shrimp, Norwegian seafood is renowned for its exceptional quality and taste. For a truly memorable dining experience, we recommend trying some of the local specialties such as gravlaks (cured salmon), lute    sk (dried sh), and rak sk (fermented sh). These dishes may sound unusual, but they are beloved by Norwegians and o    er a unique glimpse into the country's culinary traditions.

If you prefer meat, Norwegian cuisine has plenty to o    er as well. Try some reindeer stew, a traditional dish enjoyed by the indigenous Sami people for centuries. For a taste of the sea and the land combined, sample fårikål, a hearty lamb and cabbage stew that is considered Norway's national dish. And don't forget to try the famous Norwegian waes, traditionally served with sour cream and jam, for a sweet treat.

When it comes to dining recommendations, Norway's cities have a vibrant food scene that caters to all tastes. In Oslo, the capital city, you'll nd a wide range of restaurants o    ering international cuisine as well as traditional Norwegian dishes. For a taste of the local fare, head to Mathallen Oslo, a food hall that features a variety of Norwegian delicacies from di      erent regions of the country.

Bergen, a picturesque coastal city, is known for its fresh seafood. Visit the iconic Fish Market, where you can indulge in a delicious seafood feast while enjoying stunning views of the harbor. If you're in Trondheim, make sure to try the city's famous sh soup, a creamy and avorful dish that is a local favorite.

Whether you're a cultural enthusiast, a nature lover chasing the Northern Lights, or a city explorer, exploring Norwegian cuisine is an essential part of your journey. From the freshest seafood to traditional delicacies, Norway's culinary o     erings will leave you craving for more. So, don't miss the opportunity to savor the magic of Norwegian cuisine during your travels through this enchanting country.

# Conclusion

## Re ection on the beauty and magic of Norway

Norway is a land of breathtaking landscapes, rich history, and vibrant traditions that captivate the hearts of all who visit. From the majestic fjords to the mesmerizing Northern Lights, this Nordic gem o     ers a truly magical experience for every traveler.

As cultural travel guides to Norway, we have had the privilege of exploring the art, history, and traditions that make this country so unique. Each corner of Norway has its own story to tell, and it is in these stories that we nd the true beauty and magic of this enchanting land.

The rst thing that strikes any traveler to Norway is the awe-inspiring natural beauty. The fjords, with their towering cli s and crystal-clear waters, create a spectacle that leaves visitors speechless. As we sailed through the Geirangerfjord, surrounded by snowcapped mountains and cascading waterfalls, we couldn't help but be overwhelmed by the sheer grandeur of nature.

But it is not just the fjords that leave a lasting impression. The Northern Lights, a phenomenon unique to this part of the world, paint the night sky with vibrant hues of green and purple. As we stood under the dancing lights, we felt a sense of wonder and awe, as if we were witnessing something truly magical.

Norway's rich history is another aspect that adds to its allure. From the Viking Age to the present day, the country has a fascinating past that is re ected in its architecture, museums, and traditions. Exploring the medieval city of Trondheim, with its ancient cathedral and charming cobblestone streets, we couldn't help but feel transported back in time.

And then there are the vibrant cities of Oslo and Bergen, where modernity meets tradition. The Oslo Opera House, with its stunning architecture and panoramic views of the city, is a testament to Norway's commitment to the arts. In Bergen, we wandered through the colorful wooden houses of Bryggen, a UNESCO World Heritage site, and immersed ourselves in the city's vibrant cultural scene.

Whether you are a cultural enthusiast, a nature lover, or a seeker of the Northern Lights, Norway o ers a journey like no other. It is a place where beauty and magic coexist, where history and traditions come alive, and where every corner has a story to tell. So pack your bags, embark on this enchanting journey, and let the beauty and magic of Norway captivate your soul.

## Encouragement to explore the diverse aspects of Norwegian culture, history, and traditions

Welcome, fellow travelers, to the enchanting world of Norway! As you embark on your journey through this captivating country, we invite you to delve deeper into its rich culture, history, and traditions. Norway is a land that holds countless treasures, waiting to be discovered by those with an adventurous spirit.

For the cultural enthusiasts among you, Norway o ers a tapestry of artistic expressions that will ignite your imagination and captivate your senses. From the haunting melodies of traditional folk music to the breathtaking works of renowned painters and sculptors, Norway's art scene is as diverse as it is aweinspiring. Don't miss the opportunity to explore the iconic Vigeland Sculpture Park in Oslo or immerse yourself in the vibrant art districts of Bergen and Trondheim.

To truly appreciate the essence of Norway, one must also delve into its storied history. From the Viking era to the modern-day, Norway's past is lled with tales of triumphs, struggles, and resilience. Journey through time as you visit historical landmarks such as the Akershus Fortress in Oslo, the ancient Bryggen Wharf in Bergen, or the Nidaros Cathedral in

Trondheim. Each of these sites carries the whispers of the past, inviting you to unravel the secrets of Norwegian history.

No exploration of Norway would be complete without immersing oneself in its cherished traditions. From the lively festivities of Norwegian holidays to the warm hospitality of its people, traditions are woven into the fabric of everyday life here. Experience the magic of Christmas at the world-famous Christmas markets, witness the thrill of the St. Olav Festival in Trondheim, or indulge in the mouthwatering avors of traditional Norwegian cuisine, such as lute sk or rak sk.

For those travelers seeking a unique and aweinspiring experience, Norway's mesmerizing Northern Lights phenomenon awaits. Venture into the Arctic wilderness, where the dancing lights of the Aurora Borealis will leave you breathless. Whether you choose to embark on a guided tour or venture out on your own, the Northern Lights will undoubtedly leave an indelible mark on your soul.

Finally, for those who crave the vibrant energy of urban life, Norway's cities o  er a captivating blend of modernity and tradition. Explore the cosmopolitan streets of Oslo, where world-class museums and cutting-edge architecture coexist with centuries-old landmarks. Wander through the colorful streets of Bergen, a UNESCO World Heritage site, and soak in the vibrant atmosphere of its famous sh market. Or lose yourself in the charming alleyways of Trondheim, where medieval history meets contemporary charm.

So, dear travelers, let your curiosity guide you as you embark on this journey through the magic of Norway. Open your hearts and minds to the diverse aspects of Norwegian culture, history, and traditions, and let this country weave its spell on you. Norway is waiting to be discovered, and its wonders are boundless. Safe travels!

# Final travel recommendations and closing thoughts

As your journey through the enchanting landscapes of Norway comes to an end, we would like to o    er you our nal travel recommendations and share some closing thoughts. Whether you are a cultural explorer, a Northern Lights enthusiast, or someone who loves exploring vibrant cities, Norway has something special to o    er to each one of you.

For our cultural travel guide to Norway, we recommend visiting the historical city of Bergen. Known for its rich heritage and UNESCO-listed Bryggen Wharf, this city will transport you back in time. Don't miss the chance to explore the vibrant art scene in Oslo, home to world-class museums like the Munch Museum and the National Gallery. For a deeper understanding of Norwegian traditions, a visit to Trondheim is a must, with its iconic Nidaros

Cathedral and the Sverresborg Open-Air Museum.

If you are a Northern Lights enthusiast, Norway provides some of the best opportunities to witness this awe-inspiring natural phenomenon. Head to Tromsø, known as the "Gateway to the Arctic," where you can embark on thrilling Northern Lights safaris. The Lofoten Islands, with their stunning landscapes and clear night skies, are another excellent destination for chasing the elusive lights. Remember to pack warm clothing, be patient, and keep an eye on the Aurora forecast for the best chances of experiencing this magical spectacle.

For those who prefer city exploration, Oslo, Bergen, and Trondheim o er a myriad of unique experiences. Explore the trendy neighborhoods of Grünerløkka and Vulkan in Oslo, lled with vibrant street art, cozy cafes, and local boutiques. In Bergen, take a stroll through the colorful wooden houses of Bryggen and visit the Fish Market for a taste of local delicacies. Trondheim, with its charming old town, is perfect for leisurely walks along the Nidelva River and a visit to the majestic Nidaros Cathedral.

In closing, we hope that your journey through Norway has been lled with unforgettable moments, breathtaking landscapes, and enriching cultural experiences. Whether you were mesmerized by the dancing Northern Lights, captivated by the historical treasures, or charmed by the vibrant cities, Norway has left an indelible mark on your travel memories. We encourage you to keep exploring, keep discovering, and keep immersing yourself in the magic of travel.

Thank you for choosing "The Magic of Norway: A Journey through Art, History, and Traditions" as your guide. Safe travels and may your future adventures be lled with wonder and joy!

Impressum

Jan Dierssen

Hammersbecker Weg 6

28790 Schwanewede

buecherjan1993@gmail.com

Milton Keynes UK
Ingram Content Group UK Ltd.
UKHW022026301123
433552UK00015B/755